get Naked in the Kitchen

Healthy RECIPES that are proud to bare it all!

BRIANA SANTORO

with fabulous contributions from:

James Colquhoun
and Laurentine ten Bosch

Alex Jamieson

Julie Daniluk

Dr. Natasha Turner

Melissa Ramos

Shannon Kadlovski

Marni Wasserman

Alicia Diaz

Connie Jeon

Tamara Green

Jesse Schelew

Ashley Anderson
and Mark Guarini

THE NAKED LABEL
undressing the food we eat

get naked in the kitchen

Copyright © 2013 by The Naked Label

All rights reserved. No part of this book may be reproduced in any form or by any electronic, photographic or mechanical means; nor may it be stored in a retrieval system, transmitted, or otherwise be copied for public or private use—except by a reviewer who may quote brief passages in a review or article, without permission in writing from the author.

undressing the food we eat

The Naked Label

56 Palmerston Ave.

Toronto, ON M6J 2J1

www.TheNakedLabel.com

The information included in this book is for educational purposes only and is not meant to be a substitute for seeking the advice of a health care professional. This information is not meant to replace modern medicines or medical treatments. The author and publisher make no claims as to the ability of the foods listed in this book to cure or treat you of any ailments known to man.

The author and publisher have made their best efforts to ensure the information in this book is accurate, however, they make no warranties as the accuracy or completeness of the contents herein and cannot be held responsible for any errors, omissions or dated material. The information given in this book may not be suitable for your situation and you should consult a professional before trying the recipes listed in this book. The publisher and author assume no responsibility for any outcome resulting in applying the information found in this book, either through self-care or under the care of a health care professional. Neither the publisher nor the author shall be liable for any damages including but not limited to special, incidental, consequential or other damages. If you have health concerns, talk to a qualified professional first.

ISBN: 978-0-9921558-0-3

Photography by Nathalie Norris

Editing by Christine Waldner and Jenny-Lou Santoro

Graphic Design by Stasia Blanco

Cover Photo by Brooke Palmer

Food Preparation for Photography by Ashley Anderson, Esther Epp, Jennifer Southward, Tim Condon, Emily Smalley, and Melissa Ziaei

acknowledgements

Written By Briana Santoro, Founder of The Naked Label

First of all, I would like to thank my husband, **Steve Santoro.** Without him this book may never have been completed. He is my rock, my biggest supporter, the love of my life, my best friend, and my official recipe taste tester. He shares my passion for making the world a better and healthier place. He is one of the most creative people I have ever met and the "idea guy" behind this project and a lot of what we do at The Naked Label. I'm so lucky to have him in my life.

I would also like to thank the dynamic duo team that helped manage this project at The Naked Label. **Ashley Anderson** and **Nathalie Norris** were the superstars behind coordination, food preparation, and photography. The effort and commitment of these two ladies has made this project a reality. Many long hours went into creating this book and I sincerely thank them for their awesome contribution.

A special thank you to the incredible group of individuals who helped with preparing the food for photography: **Ashley Anderson, Esther Epp, Jennifer Southward, Tim Condon, Emily Smalley,** and **Melissa Ziaei.** This involved very long days, creativity, and high energy. They were amazing! One look at the food in the pictures throughout the book and you will see what an incredible job they did.

To the brilliant Holistic Nutritionists who helped write the nutritional benefits: **Chloe Elgar,** and **Semhar Ghedela.** Their expertise and support has been invaluable. They make learning fun and they do a great job illustrating how beneficial these recipes are for our health.

To my incredible graphic designer **Stasia Blanco** for making this book look so incredibly beautiful. To my cover photographer **Brooke Palmer** for making me feel comfortable and being so committed to capturing the perfect photo. To **Bree Powell** for helping me look and feel my absolute best.

To my parents, **Jennifer and Ken Southward,** for always feeding me healthy food and for introducing me to whole foods at a young age. They have been the inspiration behind my journey and I am forever grateful for their guidance and support. I also want to thank them for allowing our team to take over their kitchen for some of our food photography days. What a great space to cook. Also a special thank you to my mom for helping with food preparation and clean up! You are amazing!

To **Rhonda Richer** and **Tim Lipa** for graciously allowing us to use their kitchen and dishes to complete a number of our food photos. The photos are what brings this book to life and we couldn't have done it without them!

To my brother **Scott Southward** for being such a good friend, for teaching me to not take life too seriously, and to have fun along the way.

To **Christine Waldner** and **Jenny-Lou Santoro** for helping to edit this book. Your editing skills are exceptional and I am so grateful to have you both in my life. A special thank you to **Vince Santoro** for your outstanding help with set design.

To the rest of my family and friends for all your support, for making my life so much fun, and for being the people who light me up every day.

And most importantly, a special thank you **to all the wonderful contributors.** Without their support and delicious recipes, this book would not exist. I am forever grateful for their excitement in this project and their creativity in the kitchen. I think that what they are all doing to help create a world where everyone can be healthy and feel fabulous is amazing.

introduction

Written by Briana Santoro, Founder of The Naked Label

Welcome to The Naked Label cookbook! Putting this project together has been a dream come true for me. Back in 2007 I decided to leave the world of Business Strategy Consulting and pursue my deep-seated passion for food. I went back to school to become a Holistic Nutritionist and have been on a mission to transform the world ever since. I'm out to create a world where everyone can be healthy and feel fabulous.

I say "can" because I believe being healthy is a choice. However, I also believe that the state of the world we currently live in makes this choice challenging. Daily we are bombarded by mixed information and messages, including from companies who prioritize profits over our health and from organizations who cater to big industry interests. The end result is that we are told we can eat anything and everything as long as we do so in moderation. Unfortunately, this advice isn't working. People are getting more and more sick, and our food system is becoming more and more damaged. I started The Naked Label because I wanted people to have access to trusted information about the food we eat; so true health can be a choice.

In 2012 I asked The Naked Label community what more we could do to help them be healthy and feel fabulous. The overwhelming majority said they wanted more recipes! This was great news for me since I had a dream of creating a cookbook. However, when choosing what kind of cookbook I wanted to create, I realized that I wanted a book that was more than just an accumulation of *my* recipes. I wanted to create something that would initiate a movement; a book that eliminates the confusion about food and what is "right" to eat. A book that shows people that eating healthy can be delicious, simple, and a boatload of fun! A book that brings families together and creates incredible friendships through scrumptious food that inspires us to connect around a dinner table. A book that creates bodies that are healthy, full of energy, youthful, and vibrant. Ultimately, a book that transforms our relationship with food. Radical idea for a cookbook? Maybe. A cookbook whose time has come? Definitely!

The first thing I wanted to tackle was eliminating the confusion about food and what is right to eat. One of the things I noticed is that people tend to be on a quest to find the 'one' right diet. (The word diet here refers to the noun which means the food we regularly consume and not to the verb which refers to a weight loss regime). This quest generally leaves people confused because they hear completely opposite viewpoints from different experts and find it challenging to know who to trust. Some experts say eat meat, some say don't; some say eat grains, some say you shouldn't; some say cook your food, while other say eat it raw. People are often left with their heads spinning. It's no wonder we keep drifting back to what we already know. The long and short of it is, they are all right. Let me explain...

What my experience has taught me about food is that we are all individuals and we are all unique. Therefore, depending on our own biological individuality, our stage of life, and any symptoms or imbalances we are dealing with, our dietary requirements may vary. The real expert is within you. At the end of the day it's not about what diet is 'right', it's about what diet is 'right' for each of us as individuals.

If you are the type of person who thrives on a raw vegan diet then it's great to find experts who can support you. If, however, you feel that eating more of a Paleo-style diet leaves you feeling the healthiest and most vital, then finding an expert to support those food choices will be helpful.

I wanted to create a book that pulled together a number of incredible experts to show off their talents and provide a safe space for people to explore food and their inner expert, to determine what feels right for them.

The natural health experts I have spoken to believe in eating a diet that consists of whole, natural foods. It is the string that ties us all together. We don't believe in processed, chemical-laden, science-created food. We believe that those kinds of foods lead to poor health and disease. Which whole, natural foods we favor and how we craft them into a meal is what varies between us.

This book is unique because it consists of recipes from 15 natural health experts. There is a wide range of experts including Holistic Nutritionists, Naturopaths, documentary filmmakers, and natural health-focused Dieticians. I wanted to show the world that while we may approach food differently, our collective wisdom can live harmoniously in one book because we share a foundational focus on whole, natural foods.

You will notice that all of the recipes in this book are made of whole, natural foods. Foods that, depending on your biological individuality, will help to create a body that is healthy, full of energy, youthful, and vibrant. So often we fail to consider the continuous and important contribution that food makes to who we become. Food is not just a substance that goes in one end and out the other. In fact, we truly are what we eat.

On a scientific and energetic level we actually become the food we eat. When we eat food, it is broken down into small components that are absorbed by the body. The body then uses these raw materials to create new cells and perform many functions. Since our cells are constantly regenerating themselves, we as humans are constantly turning into the food we are eating. So it begs the question... Do we want our bodies to be made of microwave dinners and unhealthy French fries? Or do we want our bodies to be made of whole, natural foods?

When you look at it this way, it's not too hard to understand why people who eat poorly experience more disease. The flip side is also true; eating healthy can help prevent disease. In fact, eating healthy in many cases can actually reverse disease. Just think about it, when your body is sick and you then eat healthy, nutritious foods, your body will be rebuilding itself with those nourishing building blocks and therefore regenerating a healthy body. One of the goals of this book is to provide you with recipes that will help create the health you desire and deserve.

Earlier I talked about how I'm creating this book to initiate a movement. I've just explained how I hope to get rid of the confusion about food by eliminating the belief that there is one right diet for everyone and encouraging you to listen to your inner expert. I've also talked about how our bodies are rebuilt with the food we eat and we therefore have the choice to create healthy or unhealthy bodies. However, the movement doesn't stop there. I want you to realize the true beauty that food can provide.

For me, food is a tool to create connection. It provides us with a way to bring the entire family together around a dinner table to share stories about the day we've had. It brings friends together. We go out and meet with friends to eat food and we welcome friends into our homes to enjoy a meal. Food is an incredible facilitator of connection. With connection comes love, fulfillment, and happiness.

In my house we all cook together. The process of preparing a meal is not a chore, it is a special time to create incredibly tasty dishes that will nourish our bodies, please our senses, and grow stronger bonds with the people who share in this experience. I hope this book inspires your creative juices and facilitates incredible experiences, memories, and laughter with those you cherish.

I believe food is the key that will create a world where everyone can be healthy and feel fabulous. This book is a part of that mission, and now you are part of that movement. Welcome to the power of food.

meet the author

Briana Santoro

CERTIFIED NUTRITIONIST
FOUNDER AND CHIEF PRODUCT UNDRESSER AT THE NAKED LABEL

www.TheNakedLabel.com

Years ago I worked in business strategy consulting and marketing. What I noticed was that many food companies focus their efforts on convincing consumers that their products are healthy, instead of creating healthy products. This frustrated me, so I started The Naked Label. I wanted to 'undress' the food we were eating to help people see past the fancy marketing and make more informed choices. At this time I realized that food was more than just a hobby. I left the consulting world and went back to school to become a holistic nutritionist. It was through this journey that I discovered the power of food.

My view on food is simple. I believe that we are all unique. There is no one right way of eating for everyone and we can listen to our inner expert when choosing the foods that are right for us. When this is done correctly, food can heal our body. I believe that food is at the centre of connection. It is a powerful tool that brings family and friends together. I believe in eating whole natural foods, the type of foods that nourish us and leave us feeling healthy and full of life. When it really comes down to it, I am on a mission to create a world where everyone can be healthy and feel fabulous. This starts with transforming our relationship with food.

meet the contributors

James Colquhoun and Laurentine ten Bosch

FILM MAKERS OF 'FOOD MATTERS' AND 'HUNGRY FOR CHANGE'

www.FoodMatters.tv and www.HungryForChange.tv

James Colquhoun

Hi, I'm James Colquhoun and I'm passionate about food! After helping my father who was 5 years bedridden and on drugs heal himself with nutrition and natural medicine, I knew what it took to turn your health around. It all started back in 2007, where with video camera in hand, Laurentine and I began work on what was to become the 'Food Matters' film. We had digested hundreds of books and concluded our knowledge with a Nutrition course through the Global College of Natural Medicine. Since that day I have been 100% dedicated to helping this lifesaving message reach the world. My focus is on helping you improve your food choices wherever you are on your journey. I believe that food should be cleansing, it should be restorative, and it should be fun! To your good health!

Laurentine ten Bosch

Hi, my name is Laurentine ten Bosch. I'm originally from Holland and having grown up in many different countries I have always had a passion for international food and culture. I studied Nutrition at the Global College of Natural Medicine and was so fascinated by what I learned I wanted to share it with the world. Instead of becoming a Nutritionist in my home town, I wanted to deliver this message to a much wider audience so I decided to make films. My husband James and I travelled around the world, interviewing many leaders in the natural health field. Our mission had no boundaries! And today our website, films, and books inspire people to not only make healthier food choices but also address chronic illness using nutritional therapy.

Alex Jamieson

CERTIFIED HOLISTIC HEALTH COUNSELOR, AUTHOR, AND CO-CREATOR OF THE DOCUMENTARY 'SUPER SIZE ME'

www.AlexandraJamieson.com

I've been into food since birth. From my mom's organic garden, to guest hosting on her organic gardening radio show when I was 7, to becoming a healthy gourmet chef and then a Certified Holistic Health Counselor, food and health have been a major part of my life.

Creativity also runs in my veins—from co-creating the Oscar nominated documentary Super Size Me to writing three books, *The Great American Detox Diet, Living Vegan for Dummies,* and *Vegan Cooking for Dummies*—every meal is a chance to create something new.

Now I spend my days helping clients love their bodies so they can love their lives, blogging, and riding my bike through Brooklyn with my 6.5-year-old son. Life is good!

Julie Daniluk

TV HOST, AUTHOR, SPEAKER, AND NUTRITIONIST

www.JulieDaniluk.com

While mastering the rigorous theatre arts program at George Brown Theatre College, I found I was reading more about nutrition than Shakespeare, and had developed an insatiable appetite for figuring out how and why food affects our health. I decided to pursue a new direction and I attended the Canadian School of Natural Nutrition to become a registered nutritionist. I then went on to become a co-op owner & Chief In-Store Nutritionist, at one of Canada's largest health food stores, The Big Carrot in Toronto, Ontario.

My book, *Meals That Heal Inflammation,* came from my own personal health crisis. While vacationing on a remote island off of Thailand, I contracted a nearly lethal dose of food poisoning that left me paralyzed from the neck down. The combination of the bacteria, and high dose intravenous antibiotics that were used to save my life, ruined my bowel lining and left me with the inability to digest most foods. I spent four years rebuilding my gut bacteria and repairing the lining of my digestive system. It took that long because I did not have a guidebook that taught me how to heal. The good news is that *Meals That Heal Inflammation* can now guide those who are experiencing chronic inflammation from a broad range of health concerns including IBS, Crohn's, fibromyalgia, allergies, skin disorders, asthma, heart disease, arthritis, and any other condition ending in "-itis".

Dr. Natasha Turner, ND

DR. NATASHA TURNER IS A REGULAR GUEST EXPERT ON THE DR. OZ SHOW, THE FOUNDER OF CLEAR MEDICINE WELLNESS BOUTIQUE, AND THE AUTHOR OF THREE INTERNATIONALLY BESTSELLING BOOKS: THE HORMONE DIET, THE SUPERCHARGED HORMONE DIET AND THE CARB SENSITIVITY PROGRAM.

www.DrNatashaTurner.com

I have been managing the symptoms of more than one hormonal imbalance for 13 years. In fact, it's the very reason that I pursued a career as a naturopathic doctor, and later developed the step-by-step process to restoring total balance that became *The Hormone Diet*. From my personal experiences and my years in clinical practice, I know that optimal insulin balance is the most important factor in living a vibrant, strong, and healthy life. If you asked me the three most important things you could do for your health right now, I would give you the following advice: improve your sleep, eat for hormonal balance, and consume a few essential supplements (such as fish oil, fiber, probiotics, and vitamin D). How simple does that sound? Surprisingly, though, the effects of implementing these basic suggestions are significant when it comes to restoring and maintaining your insulin balance, achieving your ideal body composition and—perhaps most important—feeling your best for the long term.

Melissa Ramos

AS A NUTRITIONIST, ACUPUNCTURIST AND OWNER OF SEXY FOOD THERAPY, MELISSA IS ALSO THE OFFICIAL HEALTH BLOGGER FOR HUFFINGTON POST AND IS A REGULAR EXPERT ON CTV'S THE SOCIAL. SHE HAS BEEN A REGULAR EXPERT ON CBC'S HIT DAYTIME SHOW, STEVEN & CHRIS AND HAS APPEARED ON CP24'S WYLDE ON HEALTH, CHUM AND VIRGIN RADIO, AND WAS NAMED WOMAN OF THE WEEK FROM WOMEN'S POST MAGAZINE.

www.SexyFoodTherapy.com

I come from a fast-paced corporate world as a previous Ad Exec, so I get the hustle. I suffered for years with a gluten sensitivity that wreaked havoc on my digestive system. I had acne and almost died from a ruptured cyst that tore off a piece of my right ovary and left me bleeding internally up to my lungs. But I came back stronger than ever with a whole new outlook on life.

Now I am a Nutritionist and Acupuncturist. I help people lose weight, get more energy, be happier and feel sexy from the inside out. I don't believe that getting healthy should be confusing, boring, or stressful. After all, you've got a lot on your plate already, don't you? I also won't ask you to give up everything you love, tell you never to cheat, or to not eat past 8pm… because I do sometimes! I'm all about yin-yang balance baby. So go ahead, be promiscuous and flirt with different eating genres and BE who you want to be without the judgment… or guilt.

Shannon Kadlovski

CERTIFIED NUTRITIONIST, HEALTHY LIFESTYLE SPECIALIST, AND AUTHOR OF GET THE GUNK OUT

www.ShannonKadlovski.com

As a former unhealthy, junk-a-holic, I understand what it's like to be overweight, tired, and fearful. My personal struggles with debilitating anxiety, chronic fatigue, and irritable bowel, leading up to my now healthy and vibrant life, is what drives me to empower others to make positive changes in their own lives. After receiving my Bachelor's degree from York University, I took my passion to the Institute of Holistic Nutrition, where I obtained my Certified Nutritional Practitioner (CNP) designation. I have made it my mission to help and educate as many people as I can about the amazing, life-changing benefits that proper diet and healthy habits can have on our lives.

My approach to health and wellness is all about living "gunk-free". It's simple—eat wholesome, natural, clean foods as much as possible and try to minimize the amount of processing and chemicals involved. Don't give up the foods you love, just choose healthier versions of them. Don't take yourself too seriously or be too hard on yourself, it's all about balance. I live my life according to these principles, and I encourage you to do the same!

Marni Wasserman

MARNI WASSERMAN IS A CULINARY NUTRITIONIST AND HEALTH STRATEGIST. SHE IS THE OWNER OF TORONTO'S FIRST PLANT-BASED FOOD STUDIO & LIFESTYLE SHOP. SHE IS THE AUTHOR OF SEVERAL WELL-RECEIVED PLANT-BASED SERIES E-BOOKS, IS A CONTRIBUTOR TO CHATELAINE, HUFFINGTON POST, VITALITY, AND TONIC MAGAZINE, AND IS THE CO-AUTHOR OF A NEW BOOK CALLED FERMENTED FOODS FOR DUMMIES.

www.MarniWasserman.com

My food journey started when I was 13 years old. I had decided that a vegetarian lifestyle was definitely of interest to me. As a teenager my staples were eggs and potatoes with ketchup, and a variety of pre-prepared foods like veggie nuggets. As the years went on there was a drive in me to learn more. My initial interest in vegetarianism was starting to shape the way I thought about the human body and how food played an important role in our health. Gradually I researched the best ways to consume whole foods in a manner that would contribute to overall vitality. This led me to become a personal trainer, a certified chef, a culinary nutritionist, and eventually influenced me to start my own business, which aims to educate people about a plant-based lifestyle.

To put it as simply as possible, I love to eat. I love to experience food and all of its nutritious wonders, but more than anything, I love to share my delicious knowledge.

Alicia Diaz

AYURVEDIC HEALTH COACH

www.AyurvedaWithAlicia.com

Food in the Ayurvedic tradition is revered as the fundamental building blocks of the 7 bodily tissues, as well as a gateway into our mind, our emotions, and even spiritual fulfillment. Food brings friends, family, and communities together and the more we can all enjoy the wholesome, nutritious taste, the greater its ability to heal us! My name is Alicia Diaz and I am a holistic health coach specializing in the ancient healing tradition of Ayurveda. One of my greatest blessings in this life is to have studied with the world-renowned Ayurvedic physicians, Dr. Vasant Lad and Dr. Pankaj Naram, who have passed this healing science down to me. Using everything I have learned from these amazing physicians, I help women overcome fatigue and stress and cultivate abundant energy and vibrant health that truly lasts. I absolutely LOVE food and use recipes and nutritional education with my clients to help them with everything from overcoming exhaustion to balancing their hormones and menstrual cycles, by unlocking the wisdom of their own bodies so they can heal from within.

Connie Jeon

AUTHOR OF "THE ALKALINE PROGRAM", CEO OF BEST LIFE BLUEPRINT, REGISTERED DIETITIAN, AND PILATES/YOGA INSTRUCTOR

www.AlkalineProgram.com

My background in psychology, nutrition, and physical therapy affords me a unique perspective. I believe in the healing nature of our bodies and it starts with what we feed the mind, body, and soul. I believe that the act of eating has become complicated because we are no longer eating food as nature intended, we are eating food-like substances that do not nourish our body. Instead, they add toxic chemicals that are not only getting us sick, but also lead to weight gain.

I believe that it is time for a revolutionary paradigm shift in the way we eat, move, and think. Most of us need to heal from the chemical abuse the current food supply delivers. We need to come back to the basics of health, eating simple, healthy, real foods, moving regularly, and thinking positive thoughts. I battled an autoimmune condition called Lupus. I've experienced what sickness means. My passion is to help the world learn how to optimize their health and thrive.

Tamara Green

CERTIFIED NUTRITIONAL PRACTITIONER, NATURAL COOK, AND CO-FOUNDER OF THE LIVING KITCHEN

www.LivingKitchenWellness.com

I am a Certified Nutritional Practitioner and Natural Cook. I specialize in coaching and cooking for clients who are recovering from, healing, and preventing cancer. I combine my knowledge of nutrition and my passion for cooking good food to work with clients to create lasting changes in their lives.

As a child I was an extremely picky eater, only eating French fries, hot dogs, hamburgers, and pizza and as a result developed a serious case of Irritable Bowel Syndrome. I was in chronic pain for 9 years until I turned to food to heal myself. After being completely symptom free since 2008, it is my passion to assist people in their health journeys to eliminate pain and suffering, and find health through good, deeply nutritious food.

I hold a BA from McGill University and I later attended The Institute of Holistic Nutrition (IHN) to become a Certified Nutrition Practitioner. I am a self-taught cook, always experimenting with different ingredients and flavors. I am the co-founder of the Living Kitchen, a collective of holistic nutritionists and natural cooks & chefs that specialize in making people feel their best.

Jesse Schelew

HOLISTIC NUTRITIONIST

www.OutToLunchCreations.com

Hi, I'm Jesse from Out To Lunch Creations. I grew up with delicious home cooked meals and developed a love for baking (and sugar) at an early age. At the age of thirteen, I decided to cut red meat out of my diet. Since my family continued to eat red meat, I experimented with simple substitutions to the family meals. In university I developed several food intolerances, the most notable being to wheat and dairy. My new diet pushed me to become more creative with my cooking and baking, thus fuelling my passion for the culinary arts. I LOVE to cook, bake, and create recipes. Over the past 15 years, it seems like I have been on millions of different diets to try to heal my digestive issues and food allergies. My healing journey has inspired me to become a holistic nutritionist so I could learn more about the healing powers of food and help people heal themselves.

Ashley Anderson and Mark Guarini

HOLISTIC NUTRITIONIST DUO

www.Tri-Fitness.org

Ashley Anderson

I love to create healthy recipes and make 'art' out of food in the kitchen. But it wasn't always bliss for me. I have been living with Inflammatory Bowel Disease (Crohn's disease) for over 17 years and since day one have been working with holistic healthcare practitioners to heal. In the early stages, I experienced many challenges when first giving my Standard American Diet a holistic nutrition overhaul. This was mainly because I found it challenging to make time for myself, for healthy food preparation, and for learning how to eat out at restaurants. I have always believed in my 'gut' that there is healing power in food and have never given up, despite some challenging times. This is where my best friend and life partner, Mark Guarini, stepped into my life. We both enrolled into holistic nutrition studies at the Institute of Holistic Nutrition. Alongside my family, Mark has been my #1 support.

Mark Guarini

Eating local, top quality whole foods is the foundation for health and physical well-being. Being a personal trainer, Olympic weightlifting and strength training coach, Reiki practitioner, fitness nutritional coach, and holistic nutritionist, I have always valued the benefits of healthy whole natural foods and pass this knowledge on to my clients. I've been immersed in the fitness and wellness industry for over 30 years and emphasize the importance of creating post and pre-workout meals using whole natural foods. For me, optimizing recovery and reducing stress is the primary focus. I believe stress is the main cause of all disease. My own personal battle with anxiety disorder along with my life-partner Ashley's struggle with Crohn's disease inspired, motivated, and led me to rediscover my love of food and the benefits of eating local organic whole foods as well as grass-fed organic protein. Taste and texture are as important to the healing process as the assimilation of food itself. Each body is different. This is why I focus on listening to your body and nourishing with colorful, delicious whole natural foods. There is nothing like the enjoyment of eating nutritious food and spending time with friends and family at the dinner table—surrounded by love.

nutrition undressed

10 TIPS FOR EATING YOUR WAY TO A HEALTHIER NEW YOU

Written by Briana Santoro

If improving your health and creating a body that is full of vitality and energy sounds exciting to you, these tips will help you get started. This is a list of the 10 guiding principles that have helped me find nutritional balance in my life. I invite you to try them out and see if they work for you too!

Remember that everyone is an individual. Learn to listen to your own body. After all, there isn't one right way of eating. The same way you would try on a new outfit to see if you want to buy it, try on new ways of eating to find out what makes you feel and look your absolute best.

Let's have some fun!

TIP 1:

DRINK LOTS OF WATER

Our sexy bodies are approximately 70% water. This makes water very important to our survival. Our body can survive for weeks without food but only a few days without water. It's needed for delivering oxygen and nutrients throughout the body, supporting elimination of toxins and waste, giving life to our cells (they die without water), can make you look younger, and many more functions. Therefore, it's extremely essential that we consume enough water throughout the day to stay healthy. Things like coffee and soda actually dehydrate us, so don't count those as water intake. A good rule of thumb is to drink half your body weight (measured in pounds) in ounces per day. Therefore, if you weigh 150 lbs you would drink approximately 75 oz of water per day. Spread your water consumption throughout the day and note that if you feel thirsty, you are already dehydrated!

TIP 2:

EAT ALKALINIZING FOODS

The Standard American Diet is filled with bread, pizza, sugar, dairy, meat, processed foods, burgers, white potatoes, cereal, soda, and coffee. It is extremely acidifying to the body. When the body is too acidic, it starts to break down and as a result unwanted symptoms and disease start to appear. An acidic diet could lead to problems like metabolic syndrome, type 2 diabetes, obesity, accelerated aging, heart disease, cancer, osteoporosis, low energy, etc. Including more alkalinizing foods like green vegetables and fresh lemon juice in the diet is a great way to help alkalize your bodily system.

TIP 3:

REDUCE SUGAR, HIGH-FRUCTOSE CORN SYRUP, AND ARTIFICIAL SWEETENERS

The process of refining sugar cane into the white, sweet substance we are all familiar with actually strips away its nutrients. Therefore, we are getting the calories and the negative effect on blood sugar, yet no nutritional value. This is bad news. Consuming too much sugar can lead to many health conditions like type 2 diabetes, high cholesterol, and heart disease. High-fructose corn syrup is also a highly processed product that is challenging for our body to digest. Artificial sweeteners like aspartame

and sucralose are also very harmful. They have been manipulated in an unnatural way and should be avoided. If you are looking to add some sweetness to your dishes, try including 100% pure maple syrup, raw unpasteurized honey, coconut sugar, or stevia (a plant that is naturally sweet).

TIP 4:

INCLUDE LOTS OF PLANT FOODS IN YOUR DIET

Plants provide a large variety of vitamins, minerals, and phytonutrients. In addition, they are loaded with fiber, which helps to keep the digestive system happy and eliminate unwanted waste and toxins from the body. When boosting plant foods in the diet, the best area to focus on is fresh vegetables. Increasing your veggie intake can have a HUGE positive impact on your health. One of the best ways to do this is to make fresh vegetable juice, another is to add greens to your smoothies.

TIP 5:

REDUCE GLUTEN AND DAIRY CONSUMPTION

Gluten and dairy consumption are two very controversial topics. The key here is to listen to your inner expert, since most people have a hard time digesting these items. If you find that you have a negative reaction or if you are in poor health, reducing or eliminating these foods may be beneficial.

Many people believe that in North America we have a gluten intolerance problem because of the way we have altered wheat. It was manipulated to increase yield and a consequence is increased gluten content. We also consume large amounts of gluten containing grains (e.g. wheat), more than most other countries. If you are looking for gluten-free alternatives try brown rice, quinoa, buckwheat, millet, etc.

As for dairy, it has been marketed as a good source of calcium, needed for healthy bones and teeth. It does contain calcium, however, dairy is also a very acidifying food (when our diet is overly acidic, minerals like calcium are leached out of our bones in order to maintain our pH balance in an alkaline state), it can result in excess mucous production, and it is difficult for many people to digest because they lack the enzyme lactase. If you are going to consume dairy, choose very high quality sources, raw if possible, and organic. Another alternative is to use goat or sheep dairy as it tends to be easier to digest than cow's dairy. Good dairy alternatives are Almond Milk (recipe on 46), Cashew Cream (recipe on page 47), coconut milk, etc. If you are worried about calcium, other fantastic sources that are more easily digested are sesame seeds, almonds, and broccoli.

TIP 6:

INCREASE FIBER

Fiber is extremely important for our health and digestion. It helps to lower cholesterol and glucose levels, and it helps to move waste and toxins through the intestines so they can be eliminated. If they are not eliminated, autointoxication (the unwanted crud sticking around in our body causing serious damage) can happen. Most people only consume about 12 grams of fiber per day, however, we should be consuming a minimum of 20–30 grams and ideally 30–50 grams per day. Since animal products do not contain any fiber, it's important to ensure you are eating high amounts of plant foods. If you are consuming grains you need to ensure they are whole grains. For example, brown rice is a whole grain and contains fiber, where as white rice is a processed grain which does not contain fiber and has had many of its nutrients removed.

TIP 7:

INCLUDE RAW FOODS IN THE DIET

It's important to include some raw foods in our diet. Raw foods are high in enzymes, which help us to digest food. They are also high in vitamins and phytonutrients, and boost our hydration due to their water content. When we heat food to high temperatures—like in cooking and pasteurization—we destroy the enzymes and some of the nutrients, and reduce the water content. Some people are able to manage eating a fully raw diet, while others feel healthier when they include a combination of raw and cooked foods. Aim to have at least 50% of your diet raw and listen to your inner expert to see what feels right for you.

TIP 8:

BUY ORGANIC, LOCAL, AND GRASS-FED WHEN POSSIBLE

Conventional farming practices today are geared towards increasing profits, not towards producing nourishing food. As a result, many harmful chemicals are used to grow our food. When we purchase organic foods we can reduce our exposure to these chemicals. We can also reduce our exposure to genetically modified foods, which may be harmful to our health.

It may not always be possible to eat entirely local, but increasing the amount of local foods we consume can be great for our health. Foods that are grown close to home don't have to be picked before they are ripe. As a result, they tend to be higher in nutrients.

Conventionally raised animal products are higher in saturated fat and lower in nutrition. They lack nutrients that are essential for our health, like vitamin K2, which is only found in animals raised on grass. Without enough vitamin K2 we are at risk for developing osteoporosis and heart disease. Aim to get high quality grass-finished meats and, when possible, get to know a farmer you trust and find out where the animals you eat come from.

TIP 9:

EAT FERMENTED FOODS

It's estimated that we have approximately 100 trillion bacteria in our digestive system. The bacteria help us digest our food, make certain vitamins, stimulate the immune system, and optimize pH levels in our digestive system so that we can easily kill disease-causing microbes. At any given time we have some good and some bad bacteria in our body. The important thing is to keep them in balance. When we eat a poor diet, drink a lot of alcohol, take antibiotics, experience high stress, are exposed to chemicals, etc, this balance can get out of whack. One of the best ways to ensure a proper bacteria balance is to eat fermented foods, which are rich in healthy bacteria. Some examples include kimchi, sauerkraut, tempeh, kombucha, yogurt, and kefir.

TIP 10:

PREPARE YOUR OWN FOOD, SHARE FOOD WITH OTHERS, AND ENJOY YOURSELF

When "industry" prepares our food for us in the form of processed, packaged, fast food, they often use a number of potentially harmful ingredients. These are chemicals, preservatives, additives, and processed ingredients that would not be found in our home kitchen. For example, do you have Autolyzed Yeast Extract, Tartrazine, Blue No. 2, TBHQ, Butylated Hydroxytoluene, Polyoxyethylene Sorbitan Monostearate, etc as ingredients in your cupboard? I sure don't! One of the best ways we can improve our overall health is to prepare our own food using real ingredients like fruits, vegetables, nuts, and seeds, as well as grains and animal foods if we consume them.

Food is incredible! It not only nourishes us, it builds connection between family and friends as we prepare and eat together. Food is supposed to be enjoyable and fun. Have fun with food, be creative, and enjoy yourself!

conversion charts

ALL CONVERSIONS ARE APPROXIMATE

LIQUID CONVERSIONS		WEIGHT CONVERSIONS		OVEN TEMPERATURES	
U.S.	Metric	U.S./U.K.	Metric	°F	°C
1 tsp	5 ml	½ oz	14 g	250	120
1 tbsp	15 ml	1 oz	28 g	275	140
2 tbsp	30 ml	1 ½ oz	43 g	300	150
3 tbsp	45 ml	2 oz	57 g	325	165
¼ cup	60 ml	2 ½ oz	71 g	350	180
⅓ cup	75 ml	3 oz	85 g	375	190
½ cup	120 ml	3 ½ oz	100 g	400	200
⅔ cup	150 ml	4 oz	113 g	425	220
¾ cup	180 ml	5 oz	142 g	450	230
1 cup	240 ml	6 oz	170 g	475	240
1 ¼ cups	300 ml	7 oz	200 g	500	260
1 ⅓ cups	325 ml	8 oz	227 g	550	290
1 ½ cups	350 ml	9 oz	255 g		
1 ⅔ cups	375 ml	10 oz	284 g		
1 ¾ cups	400 ml	11 oz	312 g		
2 cups	475 ml	12 oz	340 g		
3 cups	720 ml	13 oz	368 g		
4 cups	945 ml	14 oz	400 g		
		15 oz	425 g		
		1 lb	454 g		

let the food journey begin!

INDEX

ACKNOWLEDGEMENTS	3
INTRODUCTION	4
MEET THE AUTHOR	6
MEET THE CONTRIBUTORS	6
NUTRITION UNDRESSED	11
CONVERSION CHARTS	14

19 breakfast

CACAO OATMEAL MUFFINS	20
SWEET POTATO AND SHIITAKE OMELET	21
CINNAMON SWEET POTATO PANCAKES	22
MINI SPINACH, PINE NUT, AND MUSHROOM QUICHE	23
PUMPKIN SPICED OATMEAL	24
AWESOME OMELET	25
COTTAGE OR RICOTTA CHEESE OATMEAL PANCAKES	26
FRUIT BAKE	27
BERRY VEGAN FIBER BOMB MUFFINS	28
QUINOA ALMOND PUFF BALL COLD CEREAL	29
WHOLE-GRAIN SOUR CHERRY HOT CEREAL	30
BLUEBERRY ALMOND SCONES	31
SPROUTED BUCKWHEAT GRANOLA	32
HIGH ENERGY FRUIT AND NUT PROTEIN BARS	33
QUINOA AND PEAR PANCAKES	34
BREAKFAST BROWNIES	35

37 beverages

PERFECT GREEN JUICE	38
SCRUMPTIOUS SUPERFOOD SMOOTHIE	39
TROPICAL GREEN SHAKE	40
GOAT YOGURT AND BLUEBERRY SMOOTHIE	41
TROPICAL BLISS SMOOTHIE	42
CHOCOLATE CHAI MINT SMOOTHIE ELIXER	43
SEXY HOT CACAO	44
BEST CHOCOLATE MILKSHAKE	45
ALMOND MILK	46
CASHEW CREAM	47
ORANGE SODA	48
SPICED GRAPEFRUIT COOLER	49
WATERMELON JUICE	50
CLEANSING LEMON WATER WITH A PUNCH	51
CHIA FRESCA ENERGY DRINK	52
DETOX TEA	53

CREAMY COCONUT CHAI TEA PARTY	54

55   snacks and appetizers

GOAT CHEESE DIP	56
HUMMUS MASALA	57
HOLY GUACAMOLE!	58
BABA GANOUSH	59
VEGAN ALMOND BASIL PESTO	60
MAMMA'S ITALIAN PESTO	61
AVOCADO PESTO	62
DUCK LIVER PÂTÉ	63
SCRUMPTIOUS SEED CRACKERS	64
SWEET CUCUMBER ROLLS	65
COCONUT MUSSELS	66
SPUNKY BAKED CHICKEN MEATBALLS	67
SEXY RICE NUT ROLLS	68
SUNFLOWER SEED DIP	69
BUTTER CHICKEN WRAPS	70
SOUR CREAM AND ONION KALE CHIPS	71
CAULIFLOWER POPCORN	72
APPLE JAR	73
FRUIT KABOBS ROLLED IN TRAIL MIX	74
CHOCOLATE CHICKPEA POWER BARS	75
APPLE PIE "ICE CREAM" (GREAT FOR KIDS!)	76
GINGER APPETIZER	77

79   salads

SPINACH, STRAWBERRY, AND CANDIED PECAN SALAD	80
RUBY GRAPEFRUIT, AVOCADO, AND FENNEL SALAD	81
EDAMAME AND AVOCADO SALAD	82
NAPA CABBAGE SALAD	83
SWEET POTATO SALAD	84
CRISPY CHICKPEA KALE SALAD	85
MEDITERRANEAN QUINOA SALAD	86
ROAST VEGETABLE SALAD WITH YOGURT DRESSING	87
RAW SWEET POTATO NOODLE SALAD	88
FRESH AND COOL QUINOA SALAD	89
'WILDLY' FABULOUS SEAFOOD SALAD	90
APPLE, ARUGULA, AND CHICKEN SALAD	91
LEAFY WALDORF SALAD	92
WATERMELON SALAD	93
KALE SLAW SALAD	94
AVOCADO CHICKEN CAESAR SALAD	95

97   soups

VEGETABLE BROTH	98
CHICKEN BROTH	99
ROASTED VEGETABLE SOUP	100

MEXICAN FIESTA SOUP	101
CHICKEN NOODLE SOUP	102
FINEST FRENCH ONION SOUP	103
SQUASH AND COCONUT SOUP	104
SPLIT PEA SOUP	105
SEAWEED SOUP WITH BLACK RICE	106
GUT HEALING TURNIP AND LEEK SOUP	107
SQUASH AND CARROT SOUP	108
SUMMER SLIMMING GAZPACHO	109
LOVELY LENTIL SOUP	110

111 sides

SWEET POTATO FRIES	112
BALSAMIC RICE AND SUMMER VEGETABLES	113
TAHINI BRUSSELS SPROUTS	114
LEMON BAKED TOFU	115
CREAMY RICE AND KALE "RISOTTO"	116
MOCK MASHED POTATOES (RICH N' CREAMY)	117
RAW ONION RINGS	118
ASIAN COLESLAW	119
OVEN ROASTED TOMATO LENTILS	120
HIGH PROTEIN SUPER GREENS SIDE DISH	121

123 vegetarian mains

GLUTEN-FREE LENTIL AND SQUASH LASAGNA	124
EASY MAC AND CHEESE	126
ROASTED VEGGIE ALMOND TART	127
RAW PAD THAI	128
VEGGIE SUSHI	129
SPICY LENTIL BURGERS	130
MEXICAN (TACO) BOWL	131
BLACK BEAN YUM TUM STEW	132
AUTUMN HARVEST CURRY BOWL	133
BROWN RICE PASTA WITH PEAS AND RICOTTA	134
DAIRY-FREE ZUCCHINI ALFREDO	135
EGGPLANT HUMMUS MEDALLIONS	136
BEET QUINOA VEGGIE BURGER	137
BAKED "TUNA" CASSEROLE	138
MUNG BEANS AND QUINOA	139
CORN AND KIDNEY BEAN CHILI	140
CURRIED CHICKPEAS WITH KALE AND QUINOA	141

143 omnivore mains

AGAVE LIME CHICKEN	144
POMEGRANATE POACHED HALIBUT	145
CHICKEN CACCIATORÉ	146
SALMON, BROWN RICE, GINGER, WASABI BOWL	147
GRILLED LEMON CHICKEN	148

HEARTY TURKEY CHILI	149
ALL DAY GRASS FED BEEF OSSO BUCO	150
ROSEMARY SALMON STEAKS	151
FISH TACOS	152
COD PICCATA	153
CRISPY CHICKEN AND LETTUCE WRAPS	154
PARCHMENT PAPER SALMON	155
SHRIMP CAKES	156
CLAY POT CHICKEN	157
PESTO SALMON	158
MEDITERRANEAN CASSEROLE	159

161 desserts

COCONUT BANANA BREAD	162
LIVING BROWNIES	163
VANILLA COCONUT MILK ICE CREAM	164
GINGERBREAD COOKIES	165
CARROT CUPCAKES	166
CHOCOLATE PUDDING POPS	167
CHERRY MACAROONS	168
SEXY CHOCOLATE TORTE	169
FIBER-RICH COOKIE DOUGH	170
DATE BLISS BALLS	171
WILD BLUEBERRY TART	172
HEMP FUDGE	173
CHIA SEED PUDDING WITH COCONUT AND VANILLA	174

breakfast

THE NAKED LABEL
undressing the food we eat

CACAO OATMEAL MUFFINS	20
SWEET POTATO AND SHIITAKE OMELET	21
CINNAMON SWEET POTATO PANCAKES	22
MINI SPINACH, PINE NUT, AND MUSHROOM QUICHE	23
PUMPKIN SPICED OATMEAL	24
AWESOME OMELET	25
COTTAGE OR RICOTTA CHEESE OATMEAL PANCAKES	26
FRUIT BAKE	27
BERRY VEGAN FIBER BOMB MUFFINS	28
QUINOA ALMOND PUFF BALL COLD CEREAL	29
WHOLE-GRAIN SOUR CHERRY HOT CEREAL	30
BLUEBERRY ALMOND SCONES	31
SPROUTED BUCKWHEAT GRANOLA	32
HIGH ENERGY FRUIT AND NUT PROTEIN BARS	33
QUINOA AND PEAR PANCAKES	34
BREAKFAST BROWNIES	35

cacao oatmeal muffins

By: Melissa Ramos

Ingredients

1 cup large oat flakes

4 heaping tbsp cacao powder

4 tbsp almond hazelnut butter

½ cup + ¼ cup unsweetened almond milk

3 tbsp chia seeds

3 tbsp maple syrup (or sweetener of your choice)

½ tsp sea salt

1 tsp coconut oil

TOPPING:

Almond hazelnut butter to spread

Directions

1. Preheat oven to 350°F.
2. Soak 3 tbsp chia seeds in ¼ cup almond milk. Stir and let sit for 2 minutes.
3. Grease 6 spots in a muffin tin with coconut oil.
4. In a bowl mix oats, cacao, 4 tbsp almond hazelnut butter, ½ cup almond milk, maple syrup, sea salt, and chia seed mixture. Once mixed, scoop into greased muffin tins.
5. Bake for 25 minutes and remove from oven.
6. Top with almond hazelnut butter before eating.

Makes 6

Note

If you want to add a bit more sweetness you can increase the maple syrup.

Nutritional Benefits

From a nutritional perspective, this is a heart meridian mojo-filled recipe. According to Chinese Medicine, oats and cacao fuel the heart meridian. Oats help to calm the nerves and the heart's spirit, while cacao's bitter quality helps to stimulate the heart.

If you're going through a rough patch, this is definitely the little piece of comfort you won't want to miss.

Story

I love these muffins because they're so easy and quick to make, plus almost all of these ingredients can be found in the average home. Versus having a sugary-rich, wheat-filled muffin, this is the healthiest and of course, sexiest alternative! It makes you feel like you're having dessert for breakfast, so you can fool even children with these. How sweet is that?

sweet potato and shiitake omelet

By: Briana Santoro

Ingredients

1 tbsp extra-virgin olive oil

½ onion, peeled and diced

8 shiitake mushrooms (1.75 oz or 50 g), chopped

½ small sweet potato, shredded using cheese shredder or shredding blade on food processor

½ tbsp tamari

1 tbsp water

2 pinches of pepper

1 green onion, chopped including the green part

2 tbsp goat feta cheese (optional)

4 pasture-raised eggs, cracked into a bowl and beaten with wire whisk until combined

Directions

1. Put olive oil in a frying pan on medium heat. Add onions and cook for 5 minutes, stirring frequently to ensure they don't burn.
2. Add mushrooms and cook for another minute.
3. Add sweet potato, tamari, water, and pepper. Stir and reduce heat to medium-low for another 5 minutes. Stir occasionally. If the sweet potato is sticking you can add a bit more water.
4. Evenly spread the sweet potato mixture on the bottom of the frying pan. Sprinkle with green onion and feta cheese. Pour the egg mixture on top and spread it out so it's evenly spaced. Put a large lid on top of the frying pan, turn heat down to low, and let cook for 15–20 minutes or until cooked through. Serve with a small side salad and enjoy!

Serves 2

Nutritional Benefits

Breakfast is a very important meal of the day. Getting started with a healthy boost of protein is a good way to help us stay full for longer. Eggs not only provide protein, they also provide omega-3 fats, which help to reduce inflammation, and vitamin K2 which helps prevent osteoporosis and heart disease. Make sure you buy the best eggs you can because most conventionally raised eggs are low in these nutrients.

Story

One weekend when we were up at the cottage, my brother-in-law and sister-in-law made a similar breakfast. It involved shredded white potato, onions, cheddar cheese, and eggs. I loved this idea so much that I decided to recreate the recipe with a holistic flair. Seeing as I love sweet potato and shiitake mushrooms so much, I decided to start there and see where it took me. The result was mind-blowing!! I now use this recipe as my go-to breakfast and it has quickly become my family and friends favorite. Even my friend Tchukon who doesn't like omelets loves this one!

cinnamon sweet potato pancakes

By: Dr. Natasha Turner

From The Carb Sensitivity Program

Ingredients

1 small sweet potato

1 whole egg

½ cup egg whites (4 egg whites)

1 tbsp plain Liberté 10% goat yogurt

1 tbsp chia seeds

½ tsp vanilla extract

½ tsp ground cinnamon

1 tsp coconut oil

Directions

1. Bake or boil sweet potato until tender. Cool slightly and remove the skin with a small knife.
2. In a medium-sized bowl, mash the sweet potato until smooth.
3. Stir in egg, egg whites, yogurt, chia seeds, vanilla, and cinnamon; mix well.
4. Lightly grease a skillet with coconut oil and place over medium heat.
5. Using 1 heaping tbsp of the sweet potato mixture for each pancake, cook pancakes, flipping when bubbles form. Remove from pan when pancakes are firm.

Serves 1

Nutritional Benefits

Sweet potatoes are an antioxidant-rich tuber that can help improve cardiovascular health. The goat yogurt not only adds a delicious richness to this recipe, it is also a good source of protein and gut-healthy probiotics. The eggs provide an additional punch of protein, the chia seeds add more fiber to the dish, and the cinnamon is a great helper when it comes to regulating blood sugar.

Story

This recipe combines three of my favorite foods—sweet potatoes, eggs, and Greek yogurt. I came up with it one day when I had limited ingredients in my house after coming home from a weeklong media tour and had to prepare a quick breakfast. Not only is it high protein, the cinnamon helps to lower insulin levels and in turn beat belly fat.

mini spinach, pine nut, and mushroom quiche

By: Briana Santoro

Ingredients

⅓ cup pine nuts

2 shallots, peeled and thinly sliced

1 tsp coconut oil

6 mushrooms, cut in half and then thinly sliced

2 cups spinach, chopped

1 tbsp balsamic vinegar

1 tsp rosemary

½ tsp thyme

3 pinches both Celtic sea salt and pepper

1 ½ tbsp goat cheese (optional)

3 organic free-run eggs

Directions

1. Preheat oven to 350°F.
2. In a muffin tin place 6 silicone inserts or lightly grease the inside of 6 muffin cups with coconut oil.
3. Place pine nuts in a pan on medium heat. Stir often and toast until lightly brown. Divide the pine nuts up between 6 muffin cups and spread evenly across the bottom of the cup.
4. Place shallots in a pan with 1 tsp coconut oil on medium heat for 3–5 minutes. Add mushrooms and sauté for another 5 minutes. Add spinach, balsamic vinegar, rosemary, thyme, salt, and pepper. Sauté until the spinach is wilted.
5. Divide up the spinach and mushroom mixture between the 6 muffin cups (placing it on top of the pine nuts).
6. Place ¼ tbsp of goat cheese on top (if using).
7. Whisk eggs in a liquid measuring cup or in something that has a spout to pour. Divide the eggs up between the 6 cups.
8. Place the tray in the oven for 20 minutes. Serve and enjoy!

Makes 6 mini quiches

Nutritional Benefits

Eggs provide a great source of protein to help you kick-start your day. Since eggs are acidic it is good to consume them with alkalinizing foods to help create balance. Spinach is a great food to help provide alkalinity! Using coconut oil to cook the veggies is fabulous because it is incredibly heat stable and doesn't create free radicals when heated.

Story

I love entertaining. I have found that I am an expert at dinner parties but I often lack ideas when it comes to brunch. I was hosting brunch at my house one day and I wanted to serve eggs. However, I wanted to spice things up a little and do something that was different from the standard ways of cooking eggs. Enter these scrumptious mini quiches! They are so easy to make and lip-smacking good. They will have your guests asking you when your next brunch party will be held.

pumpkin spiced oatmeal

By: Tamara Green

Ingredients

½ cup oats

2 tbsp chia seeds

⅓ cup mashed pumpkin

½ tsp cinnamon

¼ tsp nutmeg

¼ tsp ground cloves

1 cup water

½ cup coconut milk (or you can use almond milk, rice milk, etc)

Handful of pumpkin seeds

Handful of cacao nibs

Handful of raisins

Maple syrup to taste

Directions

1. Combine the oats, chia seeds, pumpkin, water, and spices in a small pot. Simmer for 3–5 minutes, until the oats are cooked.
2. Pour into a bowl. Drizzle maple syrup and coconut milk over top. Add the pumpkin seeds, cacao nibs, and raisins.

Serves 2

Nutritional Benefits:

Thanks to the oats, pumpkin, and chia seeds, this is a gluten-free fiber-rich breakfast. It's also a good source of vitamin A, essential fatty acids, and manganese.

Story

We love granola and oatmeal but sometimes it can get a little bit boring to eat the same classic bowl of oats all the time. When we want an extra delicious breakfast that is warming, comforting, and soothing, this recipe is great. This recipe was made for fall, since we absolutely love pumpkin spiced dishes at that time of year.

awesome omelet

By: Dr. Natasha Turner

From The Hormone Diet

Ingredients

1 tbsp extra-virgin olive oil

¼ cup diced green bell pepper

¼ cup diced red bell pepper

A few slices of red onion, chopped

½ cup sliced mushrooms

1 large omega-3 egg

3 large egg whites

2 tsp crumbled goat cheese

1 slice rye toast (optional)

Directions

1. Heat the olive oil in a small skillet over medium heat. Add the green and red peppers, onion, and mushrooms. Sauté until the vegetables soften.
2. Meanwhile, beat the egg and the egg whites with a wire whisk in a small bowl until blended.
3. When the vegetables are soft, transfer them to another bowl and set aside.
4. Pour the egg mixture into the skillet and cook several minutes over medium heat until the eggs are set.
5. Spread the vegetables evenly on one side of the cooked egg, top with the goat cheese and using a spatula fold the omelet in half over the vegetables. Enjoy with a piece of rye toast (optional).

Serves 1

Nutritional Benefits:

The egg whites provide a concentrated protein and the yolk is a fantastic source of fat-soluble vitamins and carotenoids, which help prevent osteoporosis and promote overall health. The veggies offer a great punch of antioxidants and the goat cheese, which is easier to digest than cow's dairy, gives creaminess to the omelet.

Story

I have eggs for breakfast almost every morning and I love coming up with a new and creative spin on an old-fashioned omelet. As an added bonus, research shows that eggs can improve appetite control and boost energy levels. You can also easily substitute different vegetables.

cottage or ricotta cheese oatmeal pancakes

By: Dr. Natasha Turner

From The Supercharged Hormone Diet

Ingredients

- 1 cup old-fashioned, slow-cooked oats
- 1 tbsp ground flaxseed or ground chia seed
- ¼ cup fresh blueberries
- ½ cup low-fat cottage cheese or ricotta cheese
- ¾ cup egg whites (6 egg whites)
- ½ tsp pure vanilla extract
- 2 tsp coconut oil

Directions

1. Combine the oats and ground seeds in a large bowl. Stir in the blueberries, cheese, egg whites, and vanilla extract.
2. Heat 1 tsp of the coconut oil in a large skillet over medium heat. Pour ¼ cup of the pancake mixture into two areas on the pan. Cook until bubbles appear on the top of the batter and the edges appear set. Flip the pancakes and cook until set in the centre.
3. Repeat using the other teaspoon of coconut oil.
4. If desired, top with 2 tsp of Eden Organic Apple Butter or ¼ cup fresh berries.

Serves 2

Nutritional Benefits

Old-fashioned slow-cooked oats are a great whole grain and whole food, rich in fiber and iron. Adding in the flaxseed or chia seed helps provide an additional rich source of fiber and they are easy on our digestive system because of their mucilaginous properties. Blueberries give us a beneficial dose of antioxidants to help fight free radicals, and the cottage cheese and egg whites provide us with some extra lean protean.

Story

A good friend of mine actually showed me this recipe years ago when I was in naturopathic college. The great thing about protein pancakes—whether you are a student or an executive—is that they are extremely portable and they can be eaten warm or cold (which was perfect since I was a student at the time). Not to mention they have the benefit of tasting like a dessert but being high enough in protein for a belly flattening breakfast!

fruit bake

By: Briana Santoro

Ingredients

1 apple (I use Red Delicious)

1 pear (I use Bartlett)

Juice of ½ a lime

1 ½ tbsp maple syrup

1 tbsp coconut oil

⅓ cup oats

¼ cup unsweetened shredded coconut

½ tsp cinnamon

10 walnut halves, chopped

Cashew cream
(optional but highly recommended)
(see recipe on page 47)

Directions

1. Preheat oven to 350°F.
2. Remove cores and chop apple and pear into ½ to 1 inch chunks (leaving the skin on). Place in a mixing bowl.
3. Stir the lime juice in the bowl with the apple and pear.
4. Add 1 tbsp of maple syrup and ¼ tsp cinnamon to the bowl and mix.
5. In a pot on medium heat melt the coconut oil. Add the oats, shredded coconut, ¼ tsp cinnamon, ½ tbsp maple syrup, and chopped walnuts. Stir and remove from heat.
6. Place the apple and pear mixture in a baking dish. Sprinkle the oat mixture on top. Cover and bake for 40 minutes.
7. Serve with cashew cream drizzled on top (optional) and enjoy.

Serves 2

Nutritional Benefits

This recipe is fiber-rich, and fabulous! The oatmeal, apple, and pear provide the fiber. The maple syrup is a great natural sweetener that is high in minerals like manganese and zinc, which help boost our antioxidant defenses, support heart health, and support prostate health in men. Plus the added boost of cinnamon helps to regulate the release of insulin and the up-take of glucose into our bloodstream. Talk about a power-packed breakfast/dessert!

Story

Truth be told, this recipe is so good I had a hard time deciding whether it belonged in the breakfast section or dessert section. I settled on breakfast because when I created it I set out to create a twist on the typical oatmeal with fruit breakfast. That being said, it's so freakin' good you could easily serve it as dessert, like a fruit crumble.

berry vegan fiber bomb muffins

By: Ashley Anderson and Mark Guarini

Ingredients

- 2 ¼ cups purified water or natural spring water
- ¾ cup chia seeds
- ¼ cup 100% pure maple syrup (We love local Canadian maple syrup!)
- 2 tsp pure almond extract
- 1 tsp pure vanilla extract
- ¾ cup almond flour
- ¾ cup coconut flour
- 1 tsp aluminum-free baking soda
- 1 tsp pink Himalayan salt, fine ground
- 2 tbsp freshly ground flaxseeds
- ½–1 cup organic blueberries, raspberries, and/or strawberries
- ½ cup extra-virgin coconut oil

Directions

1. Preheat oven to 350°F.
2. Make 12 'vegan eggs': mix chia seeds with purified water. Let stand for 20 minutes and watch chia seeds expand.
3. In a separate bowl, combine wet ingredients: maple syrup, almond extract, vanilla extract, and chia seed mixture.
4. In another separate bowl, combine all dry ingredients: almond flour, coconut flour, baking soda, salt, ground flaxseeds, and berries.
5. Slowly combine dry ingredients with wet ingredients and mix well.
6. Using a double boiler, melt coconut oil until it becomes a liquid (about 1–2 minutes). Combine coconut oil with mixture.
7. Spoon into silicone muffin trays, muffin tins greased with coconut oil, or your favorite muffin liners.
8. Bake for 18–20 minutes. Let cool and enjoy with your favorite cup of herbal tea.

Makes 12 muffins

Nutritional Benefits

These "Mighty Muffins" are vegan, dairy-free, gluten-free, wheat-free, grain-free and white sugar free. They are loaded with healthy fiber that calms and soothes the entire digestive tract as it moves through—a great 'mucilaginous' fiber source for those with IBS or digestive disorders. How amazing is that?! These fiber bombs are loaded with chia seeds containing high amounts of healthy omega-3 fats and antioxidants. They're also a great source of vitamin E, and alkalizing minerals like calcium and magnesium. Coconut flour is a rich source of L-glutamine and helps strengthen the immune system, reduce infections, is needed for normal brain function, and is food for the cells lining the digestive tract.

Story

The love of my life, Mark Guarini, created the Mighty Muffin several years ago, made with 12 organic eggs! Everyone loves them. Recently I was asked for a vegan version to feature on a health show. Mark and I didn't think this was possible. One evening, I made a vegan 'egg substitute' (aka chia seeds soaked in water), and then decided to turn Mark's Mighty Muffins into Ashley's Berry Vegan Fiber Bombs. Mark and I love them. They're super moist, easy on my digestion, and a must try!

quinoa almond puff ball cold cereal

By: Melissa Ramos

Ingredients

½ cup quinoa puff cereal

2–3 tbsp raw almond butter

2 tbsp cacao nibs

2 tbsp hemp hearts

1 tbsp chia seeds

¼ tsp cinnamon

¼ tsp stevia (or more depending on your taste)

Couple pinches sea salt

TOPPING

Sliced strawberries

MILK

Unsweetened almond milk

Directions

1. Mix all ingredients together (except for the topping and milk) and add in more almond butter if needed to get a bally crumble.
2. Slice strawberries on top and add in unsweetened almond milk.

Serves 1

Note

Puffed millet cereal works well too.

Nutritional Benefits

From a nutritional perspective, quinoa is one of the very few complete sources of vegetarian protein. Every breakfast should begin with protein and fiber. This is helpful for regulating blood sugar. Thanks to the nuts and seeds in this dish it is a fantastic source of both.

Story

I actually came up with this recipe by mistake. I was attempting to make truffles (which I'm sure could still work if you add more nut butter), but I used the crumblings and left over little balls, added the remaining ingredients above and of course the milk. It quickly became the tastiest sugar-free and gluten-free breakfast I've ever had.

whole-grain sour cherry hot cereal

By: Ashley Anderson and Mark Guarini

Ingredients

¾ cup brown rice, quinoa, or any gluten-free *whole grain* of your choice, rinsed

⅓ cup dried sour or black cherries, soaked for 20 minutes

¼ cup hemp seeds or chia seeds (for added fiber and thickness)

¼ cup slivered almonds

2½ cups + ½ cup of your favorite dairy-free milk (e.g. almond milk, hemp milk, rice milk)

2 tbsp 100% pure maple syrup

1 tsp pure almond extract

1 tsp fresh ground flaxseed—for garnish (optional)

⅛ tsp nutmeg

½ tsp cinnamon

1 pinch of Celtic sea salt

Directions

1. Over high heat, bring 2½ cups dairy-free milk to a boil. Add your whole grain, nutmeg, cinnamon, salt, and almond extract and reduce to a simmer. Cover and let cook for 40–45 minutes (depending on cooking time for the individual whole grain used).
2. Turn heat off, uncover, and let sit for 5 minutes.
3. Transfer mixture into a bowl. Mix in cherries, slivered almonds, maple syrup, hemp or chia seeds, and garnish with ground flaxseed (optional).
4. Top with remaining ½ cup dairy-free milk. Dig in with your favorite utensil and enjoy!

Serves 4

Health Benefits

Brown rice is high in thiamine, niacin, and vitamin B6, all great nutrients for combating stress, lowering cholesterol, and helping to regulate hormones. Black cherries are an amazing food for relieving and reducing symptoms of gout, arthritis, and even exercise-induced muscle damage. This cereal is great for supporting healthy arteries and cardiovascular health: high in fiber and a good source of niacin, magnesium, and cinnamon (which helps reduce inflammation).

Story

While Mark and I were touring a local winery in Niagara-on-the-Lake, Ontario, a handsome 85-year-old man approached me. He started up a conversation with me, telling me all about his winery and his love of wine. He told us about his love for respecting the environment and finding ways to use every part of the grape so that there is no waste, including the skins and seeds. During our conversation he opened up about his gout. I told him how good sour cherries were for gout. It just so happens that his brother has a black cherry farm! Bingo! We created this recipe to inspire others to use cherries. Try enjoying this with fresh black cherry juice!

blueberry almond scones

By: Jesse Schelew

Ingredients

- 2 cups almond flour
- ¼ tsp salt
- ½ tsp baking soda
- ½ cup almonds, chopped
- ½ tsp cinnamon
- ½ tsp ginger
- 2 tbsp coconut oil
- ½ tsp vanilla
- ¼ tsp almond extract
- 1 large egg OR for vegan scones use egg substitute made with 1 tbsp ground white chia seeds and 3 tbsp warm water
- ⅛ tsp liquid stevia
- ½ cup blueberries

Directions

1. Preheat the oven to 350°F.
2. If using egg substitute, grind 1 tbsp chia seeds and mix with 3 tbsp warm water, then set aside to gel.
3. In a large bowl mix the almond flour, salt, baking soda, almonds, cinnamon, and ginger.
4. If using an egg whisk until frothy. In a separate bowl mix the coconut oil, vanilla, almond extract, egg or egg substitute, and stevia.
5. Add the wet ingredients to the dry ingredients and stir until just mixed, then fold in the blueberries.
6. Form the dough into a ball and transfer onto a large piece of parchment paper. Flatten the dough into a large 2 cm thick circle and cut into 8 wedges. Transfer the parchment paper onto a baking sheet, arrange the wedges so they are evenly spaced and trim any excess parchment paper.
7. Place in the oven and bake for 15 minutes, or until the edges are golden and a toothpick inserted in the center comes out clean.

Makes 8 scones

Nutritional Benefits

These gluten-free and dairy-free scones are very high in fiber. They are also very low on the glycemic index and won't spike your blood sugar. This is because they are sweetened with stevia, which is an herb that has a natural sweet flavor but does not actually contain sugar. Furthermore, the blueberries help provide a boost of antioxidants and phytonutrients.

Story

Growing up my mom used to make homemade scones for my sisters and me on the weekend for breakfast. They were definitely one of my favorite treats! Since I love them so much, I set out to make a scone recipe of my own that was gluten-free, dairy-free, sugar-free, and loaded with fiber. Success!! These little treats are healthy and delicious. The best part about them is that they are so versatile. You can totally change the flavor by playing around with the fruit (e.g. use rhubarb) or the nuts (e.g. use macadamia nuts).

sprouted buckwheat granola

By: Briana Santoro

Dry Ingredients

3 cups buckwheat, sprouted

1 cup sunflower seeds

½ cup flaxseed

2 cups unsweetened coconut flakes

1 ½ tsp cinnamon

½ cup ground flax

3 tsp spirulina

Wet Ingredients

2 tbsp coconut oil

2 tbsp olive oil

2 tbsp flaxseed oil

1 cup honey

½ cup filtered warm water

Directions

Sprouting instructions: To sprout the buckwheat, soak the groats overnight in water. In the morning, strain the water and rinse them thoroughly leaving them in the bowl without water for approximately 2 days, rinsing them morning and night. You will see small little tails start to grow indicating they are sprouting and ready for granola.

1. Mix all the dry ingredients in a bowl. Then, mix all the wet ingredients in a separate bowl. Now mix the wet and dry ingredients together.

2. Spread the mixture out on Teflex sheets in your dehydrator. Dehydrate at 115°F for approximately 8–10 hours. Put the granola into a glass container and store it in the fridge.

Makes 13 cups

Note

If you don't have a dehydrator, you can use your oven. In batches put the granola on a cookie sheet and bake at 250°F for 4–6 hours, or until crispy. To speed up the process you can increase the temperature slightly, however, increasing the temperature will result in the loss of some nutrients. For example, certain enzyme and vitamins do not like the heat!

Nutritional Benefits

When it comes to grains, sprouting them is like adding magic. Sprouting grains activates certain enzymes that are beneficial, while also de-activating the anti-nutrients. In addition, sprouting grains makes the nutrients within them more bio-available, and makes them easier for your system to digest! The exciting addition of spirulina is what gives this cereal its super cool green color that kids love! Spirulina is a blue-green algae that is considered a superfood because it is so jam-packed with nutrients and antioxidants.

Story

One of the things I quickly realized as a nutritionist is that most cereals on the market today, including ones that market themselves as being healthy, are not healthy. I set out to create a recipe that would provide the morning crunch I desired, fuel my body, and not leave me feeling sluggish, hypoglycemic, and hungry. This recipe definitely does the trick! I love it so much I often pack some up in a baggie to take with me in my purse for when I get the munchies throughout the day.

high energy fruit and nut protein bars

By: Ashley Anderson and Mark Guarini

Ingredients

2 large red apples, cored and chopped into small pieces

2 cups cooked hulled barley or brown rice (gluten-free option)

½ cup raw almonds or pecans, chopped

¼ cup unsweetened shredded coconut

1 oz (1 scoop) of your favorite low-carbohydrate whey protein powder (or vegan complete protein powder)

1 tbsp fresh ground cinnamon

1 tbsp fresh ground flaxseed

¼ tsp Celtic sea salt

2 organic free-range eggs, whisked

1 cup full-fat coconut milk

4 tbsp 100% pure maple syrup

1 tbsp chia seeds, soaked in 3 tbsp purified water

1 tsp pure vanilla extract

1 tsp pure almond extract

Directions

1. Preheat oven to 350°F.
2. In a large bowl combine dry ingredients: apples, cooked barley or brown rice, almonds or pecans, shredded coconut, protein powder, cinnamon, ground flaxseed, and salt.
3. In a separate bowl combine wet ingredients: whisked eggs, coconut milk, maple syrup, soaked chia seeds, vanilla extract, and almond extract.
4. Slowly combine the wet ingredients into the dry ingredients, mixing well.
5. Pour mixture evenly into an 11"x 7" pan lined with parchment paper. Bake for 40 minutes or until done. Test with a toothpick, making sure the toothpick is clean when pulled out.
6. Let cool for 15–20 minutes. Cut into bars.

Serves 6–8

Note

Bars can be wrapped in parchment paper (we like to seal ours with recycled birthday or holiday ribbons) and stored in an airtight container in the fridge for up to 1 week. For sporting events, picnics, or gift-giving, we make larger batches in advance and freeze for up to 2 months.

Story

Ash and I were looking to start the day with a high-energy snack that would provide plenty of wholesome nutrients to support our training for the Great Canadian Death Race, a 125km relay through the mountains in Grande Cache, Alberta. As holistic nutritionists, we wanted to bring homemade snacks to refuel when our bodies ran out of energy. We got creative in the kitchen and put together the essential ingredients we wanted and voilà, a bar is born! This has become our go-to snack and meal-replacement when we're on the go. We love them so much that we make 2–3 batches, wrap them up in parchment paper, and tie them with twine or pink ribbons (ash loves pink!). They're always ready when we're in a pinch and need a quick snack.

Nutritional Benefits

These high-energy fruit and nut protein bars are high in blood sugar regulating fiber, high in complete protein, and high in healthy fats that help burn calories. Apples are a great source of pectin fiber, chromium, and quercetin. Quercetin is great for reducing inflammation and histamine in the body (great for allergies!). These bars also make a great meal replacement. Why settle for store bought protein bars (full of preservatives) when you can make your own?

quinoa and pear pancakes

By: Briana Santoro

Ingredients

PANCAKE

½ cup quinoa

½ cup brown rice

Water for soaking quinoa and brown rice

1 cup unsweetened hemp milk (almond milk will work too)

½ cup unsweetened coconut flakes

1 tsp vanilla extract

1 ripe Bartlett pear, chopped with the core removed

1–2 tsp coconut oil

PANCAKE TOPPER

2 tsp flaxseed oil

2 tsp honey

½ cup raspberries

½ cup blueberries

Directions

1. Soak quinoa and brown rice in water overnight. Strain water and rinse in the morning.

2. Put the strained quinoa and rice, hemp milk, coconut flakes, vanilla extract, and pear into a high-speed blender. Blend until smooth.

3. Heat an electric skillet or frying pan on medium heat. Coat the bottom of the pan with some coconut oil. Add the pancake batter, making 3 to 4 small pancakes. When they start to create bubbles on the top, flip them over and cook the other side until golden brown. Repeat until the batter is finished.

4. To make the pancake topper, add all ingredients to a food processor (or blender) and pulse until well chopped and combined (make sure to leave some small chunks). Place on top of your pancakes and they are ready to eat.

Serves 2

Note

You can also use banana instead of pear. Use 1 ½ organic bananas (if it's a conventional banana it may be larger and you may only need 1)

Nutritional Benefits

Soaking the quinoa helps to make it soft so it blends easily but it also makes the nutrients more bioavailable and makes the quinoa more digestible. Adding berries on top is a fabulous way to get your boost of antioxidants in the morning. Not only are berries beautiful and colorful, their colors represent all of the amazing phytonutrients that they contain. In addition, berries are a great low glycemic fruit in the morning, so they will give you an excellent boost of energy without spiking your blood sugar.

Story

What kid doesn't love pancakes! I'm all grown up now and I still love them! Growing up, pancakes were the special treat my grandfather used to make my brother and I on the weekend when he and my grandmother were babysitting. Therefore eating them today brings back so many wonderful childhood memories. I set out to create a healthy recipe that would give me this treat in a gluten-free, fiber and nutrient rich way that didn't spike my blood sugar. Success! This recipe will have you licking your plate and asking for more!

breakfast brownies

By: Jesse Schelew

Ingredients

½ cup almond flour

19 oz (540 ml) can black beans, drained and rinsed or 2 cups cooked black beans

3 eggs (separate the yolks from the whites)

1 cup cacao powder

½ cup unsweetened applesauce

¼–½ cup pure maple syrup

1 tsp baking powder

1 tsp vanilla extract

¼ cup almond butter

½ tbsp cinnamon

½ cup almond milk

½ cup almonds, chopped

½ cup cacao nibs

½ cup goji berries

Note

For a low-glycemic option you could use 2 tsp of stevia powder instead of the maple syrup. Please note that this will change the flavor of the brownies.

Directions

1. Preheat oven to 350°F and line an 8" x 8" baking pan with parchment paper.
2. Whip egg whites in a small bowl until peaks form and then set aside.
3. Place the almond flour, beans, egg yolks, cacao, applesauce, maple syrup, baking powder, vanilla, almond butter, cinnamon, and almond milk in a food processor and blend until smooth. The batter will be very thick.
4. Add the egg whites, ¼ cup chopped almonds, ¼ cup cacao nibs, and ¼ cup goji berries to the food processor and process until just mixed.
5. Transfer into the pan and even out the top with a wet spatula. Sprinkle the remaining ¼ cup chopped almonds, cacao nibs, and goji berries over the brownies and gently press into the batter.
6. Bake the brownies for 35–40 minutes or until a toothpick inserted into the centre comes out clean.
7. Cool before slicing and enjoy!

Makes 12 brownies

Nutritional Benefits

Most brownies are made with grains. These brownies are amazing because they are predominately made with almonds and black beans! This combination provides loads of fiber, healthy monounsaturated fats, and protein. Adding in some cacao nibs and goji berries tops these brownies off with superfood goodness! These superfoods provide a great source of antioxidants.

Story

Brownies are typically a dessert food, and for good reason! Most brownies are unhealthy, loaded with sugar, and low in fiber. One day when I was in a creative mood I decided to see if I could create a brownie recipe that was delicious enough to be eaten for dessert, yet healthy enough for breakfast. This recipe is the result of my kitchen magic!

beverages

PERFECT GREEN JUICE	38
SCRUMPTIOUS SUPERFOOD SMOOTHIE	39
TROPICAL GREEN SHAKE	40
GOAT YOGURT AND BLUEBERRY SMOOTHIE	41
TROPICAL BLISS SMOOTHIE	42
CHOCOLATE CHAI MINT SMOOTHIE ELIXER	43
SEXY HOT CACAO	44
BEST CHOCOLATE MILKSHAKE	45
ALMOND MILK	46
CASHEW CREAM	47
ORANGE SODA	48
SPICED GRAPEFRUIT COOLER	49
WATERMELON JUICE	50
CLEANSING LEMON WATER WITH A PUNCH	51
CHIA FRESCA ENERGY DRINK	52
DETOX TEA	53
CREAMY COCONUT CHAI TEA PARTY	54

perfect green juice

By: James Colquhoun and Laurentine ten Bosch

From The Food Matters Recipe Book www.FoodMatters.tv

Ingredients

- 3 celery stalks
- 1 Lebanese cucumber
- 2 stems of kale
- ¼ fennel bulb
- 1 lemon, peeled
- 1 green apple
- ½ inch slice of ginger

Directions

1. Put all ingredients through your cold-press or conventional juicer. Have straight away but sip slowly!

Tip

This juice recipe works well with the addition of parsley and cilantro (coriander). Be generous and juice in either of these herbs by the handful.

Note

Make sure to get your celery organic, if nothing else, as conventional celery is renowned for being heavily laden with chemical residues.

Nutritional Benefits

This juice is an excellent source of easily digestible alkaline minerals, such as potassium, which is particularly helpful when cleansing. Adding in the additional herbs is great for boosting the health benefits. These are very powerful natural green plant foods for detoxifying our bodies of heavy metals.

Story

This is our all-time favorite morning youth elixer; as tasty as it is alkalizing and nourishing.

scrumptious superfood smoothie

By: Shannon Kadlovski

Ingredients

1 cup water or coconut water

1 scoop protein powder (or 2 tbsp if it doesn't come with a scoop)

1 tbsp chia seeds

1 tsp matcha green tea powder

1 tsp fish oil

1 tsp manuka honey or raw honey

½ cup fresh blueberries

Directions

1. Toss all of the ingredients into a blender and blend until smooth and creamy!

Note

For protein powder, make sure to choose one made without refined sugar or artificial flavors/sweeteners.

Serves 1

Nutritional Benefits

This super-powered, nutrient-rich smoothie will provide you with long-lasting energy to take on the day. It provides healthy fat, fiber, carbohydrates, and protein, which is everything you need in a snack or meal. The coconut water is packed with potassium and helps to hydrate the body, while replenishing electrolytes. The blueberries and matcha green tea powder are both concentrated sources of antioxidants. Furthermore, the chia seeds and fish oil provide a healthy dose of omega-3 fats, known to reduce inflammation.

Story

Smoothies are one of the best ways to start the day. Not only are they quick to make, they also provide all of the nutrients you need to kick-start your morning, in one glass. I particularly like this smoothie recipe because it's naturally sweet. The coconut water and blueberries provide a sweet taste, so all you really need is a drop of honey for extra sweetness (and in some cases, I don't even add the honey). Also, the chia seeds add a bit of thickness to it, which I really like.

tropical green shake

By: Melissa Ramos

Ingredients

1 cup coconut water

½ cup frozen mango

Juice of 1 lime

½ banana

1 handful spinach and kale

1 oz (30 ml) E3Live or green superfood powder of your choice

1 tsp chia seeds

1 scoop of vanilla protein powder (optional)

Directions

1. Mix it all together in a high-powered blender and enjoy.

Serves 1

Nutritional Benefits

Nutritionally, this shake is alkalinizing, which is needed after waking up to an acidic body. It helps to fuel the Liver meridian according to Chinese Medicine, reducing feelings of frustration and anger. In addition, the coconut water is the most natural electrolyte replacement on the planet. So with the added protein, this is an amazing post-workout recovery drink.

Story

This shake is one of my favorites. I've added the protein powder as an optional ingredient because for some, combining fruit and protein simply doesn't digest well. The great thing that I love about shakes is their versatility. My mornings are chaotic. This provides me with the fuel I need to start my day right.

goat yogurt and blueberry smoothie

By: Dr. Natasha Turner

From The Supercharged Hormone Diet

Ingredients

1 serving whey protein isolate

½ cup plain Liberté Goat Yogurt

½ frozen banana

½ cup frozen blueberries

1 tbsp chia seeds

½ cup water

Directions

1. Combine all the ingredients in a blender and purée on high speed until smooth.

Serves 1

Nutritional Benefits

This goat yogurt and blueberry smoothie is a great way to get a punch of antioxidants, complete protein, and gut rejuvenating probiotics. The complete amino acid protein profile that comes from whey protein isolate provides muscle recovery nutrients and helps build the enzyme stores in our body. The banana provides a sweet and creamy texture that feeds our body with potassium, an important electrolyte.

Story

On my patient days I can often see up to 17 people in a row—which certainly doesn't leave a lot of time to prepare and eat lunch, despite the beautiful kitchen we have at Clear Medicine. So we keep a magic bullet at the clinic and stock the fridge and cupboards with the essential smoothie ingredients. The staff is always creating fantastic new recipes and this is one of my favorites.

tropical bliss smoothie

By: Jesse Schelew

Ingredients

¾ scoop of vanilla protein powder (I recommend Sunwarrior Protein)

2 cups almond milk, more if required

⅓ cup frozen mango

⅓ cup fresh pineapple

½ banana, frozen

Handful of spinach

Directions

1. Blend and enjoy!

Serves 1

Nutritional Benefits

Mangoes are very concentrated with vitamin A, and are a good source of vitamin C. Pineapples contain a digestive enzyme called bromelain. This is great for those who have trouble digesting their food properly or experience bloating. Bromelain also has anti-inflammatory properties, which is beneficial because so many health conditions we experience today are due to inflammation. Topping this smoothie off with spinach adds vitamin K and magnesium, plus helps to alkalinize our bodies!

Story

I was recently on vacation in Maui and absolutely fell in love with this tropical paradise. When I was there, I often enjoyed delicious smoothies made with fresh fruit. Mmm just thinking about the sweetness and flavor of fresh fruit brings a smile to my face. When I returned, I wanted to create a smoothie that would instantly transport me back there just by closing my eyes and taking a sip. My suggestion for you is to put on some tropical music, whip up this smoothie, close your eyes, and sip your way to paradise!

chocolate chai mint smoothie elixer

By: Marni Wasserman

Ingredients

2 cups steeped warm or room temperature herbal tea (I use Chaga Chai tea but you can use another herbal tea or your favorite Rooibos variety)

1 scoop chocolate or vanilla vegan protein powder (I recommend Sunwarrior Protein powder)

1 frozen banana

1 tbsp goji berries

1 tbsp cacao powder

1 tbsp coconut nectar

1 tbsp coconut oil/butter

1 tbsp almond butter

1 tbsp Ormus Supergreens (or another favorite greens powder)

1 tbsp chia seeds

Directions

1. Place all ingredients in a high-powered blender and blend until warm, smooth, and creamy. Serve and enjoy!

Serves 2

Nutritional Benefits

Even though they are thick, smooth, and creamy, smoothies don't always have to be cold. They can be served warm as well! Herbal teas provide a lot of beneficial health benefits. Using an herbal tea as the base for the smoothie instead of water helps to add an extra boost of nutrition. The goji berries provide beta-carotene, the cacao powder provides antioxidants to help prevent illness, the coconut oil and almond butter provide healthy fats, and the greens provide alkalinizing nutrients that feed our cells.

Story

This recipe was created out of the desire to make my chocolate smoothies just a little bit different. I am a big fan of chai tea but don't like black tea, so I figured getting my "caffeine" from chocolate was a much tastier option!

sexy hot cacao

By: Melissa Ramos

Ingredients

1 cup unsweetened almond milk

1 tbsp tahini paste

2 tbsp cacao powder

2 tsp coconut sugar

1 tsp of maca powder

½ tsp ground chia seed

Directions

1. Heat up the almond milk and stir in tahini. Bring to a boil, remove from burner and whisk in remaining ingredients and serve.

Serves 1

Nutritional Benefits

I love this calcium rich, fiber full cup of goodness. The raw cacao is packed with magnesium, which is needed by many women before their period—now does it make sense why you crave chocolate beforehand? Adding in the maca powder (a healthy root that is grown in Peru) is a great boost of energy plus a hormone balancer. And lastly, instead of using a high-glycemic sugar, why not go for coconut sugar that's low on the glycemic index and also an incredible nutritive.

Story

There are so many times that I crave hot chocolate and that snuggly-comfort that only a cup of love can bring. This hot little number does just that, with a creamy and silky finish that leaves you feeling full. So when I'm craving something sweet and maybe even a bit dirty, I opt for this incredible healthy alternative instead.

best chocolate milkshake

By: James Colquhoun and Laurentine ten Bosch

From The Food Matters Recipe Book www.FoodMatters.tv

Ingredients

2 cups milk of choice
(for example: nut milk, coconut milk, or organic dairy)

2 heaping tbsp raw cacao powder

1 tbsp coconut oil

½ tsp ground cinnamon

½ tsp natural vanilla extract

Pinch of unrefined sea salt

2 tbsp pure maple syrup or raw honey

6 ice cubes

Directions

1. Blend everything in your blender until well combined and frothy. Enjoy straight away.

Note

For "pink milk", omit the cacao and cinnamon and blend with 10 fresh or frozen strawberries.

Serves 2

Nutritional Benefits

The raw cacao powder is a superfood that is extremely high in magnesium. The magnesium helps to lower blood pressure and prevent heart disease. The cacao is also a fantastic source of antioxidants including vitamins A, C, and E. These antioxidants can help decrease sickness and boost energy. The coconut oil is a great source of medium chain fatty acid and therefore provides quick energy for the body.

Story

In our opinion this really is the best chocolate milkshake... and let's be honest, who doesn't love chocolate milk? For a traditional 'milk and cookies' snack, try this with the Gingerbread Cookies on page 165.

almond milk

By: Briana Santoro

Ingredients

1 cup almonds

3 cups filtered water + more water for soaking

OPTIONAL

Sweetener: ½ tbsp honey OR ½ tbsp maple syrup OR 2 Medjool dates (with the pits removed) OR 5 drops stevia

Flavoring: ½ to 1 tsp vanilla extract

Directions

1. Soak the almonds overnight in water. Strain in the morning and discard soaking water.
2. Place the soaked almonds, 3 cups of filtered water, and any of the optional ingredients you are using in a blender and blend until well blended and smooth.
3. Pour the liquid into a nut milk bag and strain. Store milk in a glass container in the fridge for up to 3 days.

Makes about 1 liter of almond milk

Note

If you don't have a nut milk bag you can use a fine sieve or some cheesecloth, however, the nut milk bag will work best.

Nutritional Benefits

Almonds are a wonderful source of protein. They are also a good source of healthy fat and they contain flavonoids that are helpful for maintaining good heart health. Filtered water is better than tap water because the harmful elements have been removed.

Story

Growing up I could never drink milk. When I did it resulted in an asthmatic reaction. Therefore, almond and other dairy free milks have become my go-to creamy white liquid of choice. To be honest, I never feel like I'm missing out. Not only do I prefer the taste of almond milk but I also realize that my body doesn't react well to cow's milk and therefore my inner expert says I should steer clear. "Thanks inner expert… You are so wise!"

cashew cream

By: Briana Santoro

Ingredients

1 cup cashews

1 cup filtered water + water for soaking

½ tsp vanilla extract (optional)

1–2 Medjool dates (with the pit removed) to add sweetness (optional)

Directions

1. Put cashews in a bowl and cover with soaking water. Soak overnight. In the morning strain and rinse.
2. Put rinsed cashews, 1 cup of water, vanilla, and dates (if using) in a high-speed blender. Blend until creamy and smooth. If it's thicker than you want it to be, just add more water.

Makes approximately 1 ¾ cups

Nutritional Benefits

Cashews are a great source of healthy fat and protein. They are high in magnesium, which helps in muscle relaxation and is very supportive towards heart health. Cashews also contain the mineral selenium, which helps with prostate health, heart health, and boosting our immune system.

Story

Not only can you create milk out of nuts, you can also create cream! If you don't consume dairy or are reducing dairy in your diet, this recipe can be one of the coolest substitutes around. The first time I had it I was blown away by how delicious it tasted. Now when I am making a recipe that uses cream, I use this instead. In this book I use it on the Fruit Bake on page 27, in the Butter Chicken on page 70, and in the Duck Liver Pâté on page 63. If I had to pick one word to describe this cream, it would definitely be decadence!

orange soda

By: Briana Santoro

Ingredients

Juice of 2 oranges

Juice of ½ a grapefruit

Juice of ½ a lemon

2 cups sparkling water (like Perrier or San Pellegrino)

2 tsp maple syrup

4 ice cubes (optional)

Directions

1. Juice the fruit using a citrus juicer (either electric or hand operated).
2. Add maple syrup and stir.
3. Divide between two glasses. Top with 1 cup sparkling water in each glass.
4. Add ice cubes if desired (2 per glass).
5. Drink and enjoy!

Serves 2

Nutritional Benefits

This beverage is filled with an abundance of vitamin C. In addition, the grapefruit contains the phytonutrient lycopene. Lycopene is a powerful antioxidant that helps to fight against free radicals, which can build up in the body. Lemons help to stimulate the digestive juices and help to alkalinize the body.

Story

One of my favorite things to do in the kitchen is create healthy recipes that substitute unhealthy alternatives. I won't name names but currently I'm thinking of an orange flavored soda that comes in a teardrop bottle. I read the ingredients and noticed that it contains high-fructose corn syrup. That is a substance I stay far away from. I thought to myself… "Briana why don't you just create a healthy orange flavored soda that tastes delicious and satisfies the craving". Perfect!! What a great idea. The thing I love about this recipe is that the ingredients are all healthy and natural, yet the taste is so good it feels like we're doing something sinfully wrong.

spiced grapefruit cooler

By: James Colquhoun and Laurentine ten Bosch

From The Food Matters Recipe Book www.FoodMatters.tv

Ingredients

3 yellow grapefruits, peeled, woody core and pips removed

½ inch ginger, peeled

1 tbsp coconut oil

1 tsp ground cinnamon

1 tsp natural vanilla extract

6 ice cubes

¾ cup of spring or filtered water

OPTIONAL

Raw honey, pure maple syrup, or stevia leaf powder to taste

Directions

1. Blend on high until smooth. Sip slowly!

Serves 2

Nutritional Benefits

Great for cleansing, weight loss, and regulating blood sugar levels. Cinnamon has great blood sugar regulating properties and when mixed with coconut oil and grapefruit, is especially effective for boosting metabolism.

Story

We love this delicious cooler. It's a great mid-afternoon refreshment on a hot day!

watermelon juice

By: Briana Santoro

Ingredients

2 cups watermelon (packed)

8 mint leaves

2 tbsp freshly squeezed lemon juice

2 ice cubes

Directions

1. Put all ingredients into a blender and blend until smooth (it doesn't take long).

Makes 2 small glasses

Tip

To make popsicles for the summer, make the recipe above but don't use the ice cubes. Place the liquid in a popsicle stick tray and freeze until solid. Makes 9–10 popsicles.

Tip

To make this more of a slushy, make the recipe above (without the ice cubes) and pour it into ice cube trays. When it is frozen, throw the ice cubes into a high-speed blender and blend until slushy (don't over blend).

Nutritional Benefits

The high amounts of lycopene in this drink make it a great anti-inflammatory beverage. Nowadays inflammation is a big problem for a lot of people and this inflammation is leading to many chronic illnesses. The lycopene actually gives the watermelon its reddish-pink color, similar to grapefruit!

Story

Water is definitely my go-to beverage of choice. However, sometimes in the summer I'm looking for something to sip on that packs a punch of flavor, is refreshing, and spruces up my usual water routine. This is especially true if I'm entertaining and looking for a healthy juice to serve; one that isn't chock full of artificial sweeteners, flavor packs, and coloring agents.

cleansing lemon water with a punch

By: Ashley Anderson and Mark Guarini

Ingredients

1 cup of warm/hot purified water or natural spring water

Juice of ½ a juicy lemon

1 chamomile herbal tea bag (we love to get our fresh chamomile from a local medical herbalist)

¼–½ tsp fresh grated ginger

1 tsp 100% pure maple syrup

⅛ tsp Celtic sea salt

1 small pinch cayenne

Directions

1. Juice the ½ lemon using a citrus juicer or a large spoon (pressing it against the inside wall of the lemon to squeeze out every last drop). Add the freshly squeezed lemon juice to 1 cup of warm/hot water.
2. Add the chamomile tea bag and fresh grated ginger, and let sit for 5 minutes.
3. Remove tea bag and add maple syrup, Celtic sea salt, and a pinch of cayenne. Stir.
4. Sit back, relax, enjoy, and be washed away by this cleansing drink. For best results enjoy first thing in the morning 20–30 minutes before breakfast, on an empty stomach.

Serves 1

Health Benefits

Not only does lemon juice give a glow to the skin when taken internally, it also helps in the production of white blood cells and antibodies in blood, which attack invading microorganisms and prevent infection. Best of all, lemon juice, especially when taken in the morning on an empty stomach, clears the digestive system and purifies the liver. Chamomile is a calming herb, while ginger helps to reduce histamine in the body produced from allergies, and also helps to soothe the stomach. Cayenne is a powerful anti-inflammatory spice!

Story

Did you know that lemon juice is great for cleaning windows and countertops? It's true. But did you ever think that lemon juice was great for cleaning the liver too? With a lifetime of having fun and at times eating dirty foods, this is a great way to wash away some of that grime and give your liver that 'lemon fresh' scent. Ash and I love to start our early mornings with this recipe on an empty stomach before we hit the gym and do 20–30 minutes of light exercise, giving our body the time and the means to cleanse from head to toe. This recipe is an excellent daily detox. Don't you just love the power of food?

chia fresca energy drink

By: Alex Jamieson

Ingredients

1 cup water

1 tbsp lemon/lime juice

1 tbsp chia seeds

1 tsp maple syrup

Directions

1. Add all the ingredients to a glass. Stir and enjoy!

Serves 1

Nutritional Benefits

Lemon juice is very rich in minerals and is alkalizing to the body. It can help support your liver by gently cleansing it and by promoting a healthy digestive tract. The fiber in the chia seeds can also help excrete unwanted toxins in the body.

Story

I need good, stable energy, daily. But the *last* thing I need is sugar, food coloring and the preservatives and caffeine that are normally found in energy drinks! That's why I created my own super-easy energy drink that you're sure to love.

detox tea

By: Alicia Diaz

Ingredients

½ tsp whole cumin seeds

½ tsp whole coriander seeds

½ tsp whole fennel seeds

1–2 cups boiling water

Directions

1. Steep seeds in 1–2 cups of boiling water and drink.

Serves 1

Nutritional Benefits

Coriander is a medicinal spice used in Ayurveda to reduce intestinal spasms, digest toxins, reduce acidity, and gently stimulate metabolism. Cumin has similar benefits to coriander and is also considered anti-nausea, promotes breast milk in nursing mothers, and is one of the best herbs to promote nutrient absorption. Fennel seed is a delicious licorice-tasting herb that is incredible for reducing gas and general nervous tension.

Story

One of the first things that drew me to study Ayurveda was digestive problems I had that no medical doctor could figure out. I was in SO much pain everyday, yet all of the tests that they did concluded that I was "fine". I wasn't willing to accept a life of pain and luckily the exact tools I needed were delivered to me through this timeless healing art, Ayurveda. THIS tea recipe has helped me so much in healing my GI tract and is wonderful for oh so many ailments! One of the best times to enjoy it as a tea is in the mid-afternoon between lunch and dinner. You can use these spices in cooking as well!

creamy coconut chai tea party

By: Alicia Diaz

Ingredients

10 cups of filtered water

1 large 3-inch piece of fresh ginger root, chopped

1 handful of cardamom pods, crushed (approximately 20 pods)

8 whole cloves

5 star anise

5 whole black peppercorns

3 cinnamon sticks

1 tbsp whole fennel seeds

3 tsp of loose leaf red or vanilla rooibos tea (or 3 tea bags)

4 cups canned coconut milk (about 2 cans)

Maple syrup to taste

Dash of cinnamon, nutmeg, cardamom, and/or allspice for garnish

Directions

1. Combine water, fresh ginger, and whole spices in a large pot and bring to a gentle boil.
2. Reduce heat and simmer for 15–20 minutes (enjoy the lovely aroma that fills your home!).
3. Remove from heat, add tea bags, and let steep for 5–10 minutes, then mix in coconut milk and maple syrup.
4. Garnish with powdered spices on top and sip away to your heart's content. This tea truly brings a warm smile from the inside out! Enjoy it!

Serves approximately 12

Nutritional Benefits

There are more benefits to these spices than I can possibly list! Coconut milk is nourishing and grounding, and the combination of spices collectively stimulates the appetite and metabolism, promotes nutrient absorption, and increases circulation in the body.

Story

Sipping a cup of warm chai brings me right back to when I was studying in India, sitting next to one of my teachers, and hanging on every pearl of wisdom that poured out of his mouth. Dr. Lad and Dr. Naram are Ayurvedic physicians but they speak with the clarity, wisdom, and devotion of a saint. These chai spices make me feel peaceful, enlightened, grounded, content, and so at home. I've served this chai recipe at gatherings and I can never seem to make enough of it! It disappears SO fast! So whether you are curling up with your favorite book and a steaming mug or sharing it with your loved ones, may this recipe bring you the same comfort and peace that it brings me.

snacks and appetizers

GOAT CHEESE DIP	56	SPUNKY BAKED CHICKEN MEATBALLS	67
HUMMUS MASALA	57	SEXY RICE NUT ROLLS	68
HOLY GUACAMOLE!	58	SUNFLOWER SEED DIP	69
BABA GANOUSH	59	BUTTER CHICKEN WRAPS	70
VEGAN ALMOND BASIL PESTO	60	SOUR CREAM AND ONION KALE CHIPS	71
MAMMA'S ITALIAN PESTO	61	CAULIFLOWER POPCORN	72
AVOCADO PESTO	62	APPLE JAR	73
DUCK LIVER PÂTÉ	63	FRUIT KABOBS ROLLED IN TRAIL MIX	74
SCRUMPTIOUS SEED CRACKERS	64	CHOCOLATE CHICKPEA POWER BARS	75
SWEET CUCUMBER ROLLS	65	APPLE PIE "ICE CREAM" (GREAT FOR KIDS!)	76
COCONUT MUSSELS	66	GINGER APPETIZER	77

goat cheese dip

By: Briana Santoro

Ingredients

10 ½ oz (300 g) soft goat cheese

4 dried figs (alternatively you can use fresh ones)

½ cup chopped pecans

¼ cup balsamic vinegar

2 tbsp honey

Directions

1. Cut the goat cheese into ½ inch slices and lay out on a serving platter.
2. Chop up the figs and pecans and sprinkle on top of the goat cheese.
3. In a jar mix the balsamic vinegar and honey. Shake vigorously until well combined.
4. Pour the balsamic mixture over the goat cheese, fig, and pecan dish. Serve with crackers (I use Mary's Crackers) and enjoy!

Serves 6

Nutritional Benefits

The great thing about goat's milk products is that if you are still keen on eating dairy, goat's milk seems to be much more compatible with the human digestive system, in comparison to cow's milk. Also, honey is a great way to add some natural sweetness. It is filled with antioxidants and has an abundance of anti-fungal properties.

Story

I have a group of girlfriends in toronto who would classify this hors d'oeuvre as their all-time favorite. I brought it to a girls' night one time and now every time I'm invited over the invitation accompanies a request to bring the favorite goat cheese dish! Let's just say, when this dish is being consumed there is a whole lot of mmmmm'ing, awwww'ing, and ooooooo'ing going on. Be prepared to fall in love!

hummus masala

By: Jesse Schelew

Ingredients

2 small garlic cloves

19 oz (540 ml) can of chickpeas, drained and rinsed

¼ cup lemon juice (1 lemon)

4 tbsp tahini

2 tbsp olive oil

1 tbsp masala

½ tbsp cumin

½ tbsp turmeric

1 tsp paprika

Pepper to taste

3–6 tbsp water

Directions

1. Place garlic in a large food processor and pulse until it is coarsely chopped.
2. Add remaining ingredients, except for the water, and process until smooth. Water will make the hummus creamier; add it slowly until desired texture is reached.
3. Serve with pita, naan, cucumbers, crackers, or simply eat with a spoon!

Nutritional Benefits

This hummus recipe is great for those who want quick and easy foods to prepare. Chickpeas contain B-vitamins, protein, minerals, and are a great addition to a vegetarian diet. Lemons are great for the liver and help with gentle detoxification. They aid in digestion and are great for keeping us regular. Another reason to enjoy this recipe regularly is because of the turmeric. Due to its active ingredient curcumin, it can decrease inflammation within the body.

Story

When I was travelling through Israel I lived on hummus! No seriously, I really lived on it. It was so delicious that I would even eat it out of a bowl using a spoon for breakfast! When I got home I set out to create a delicious hummus recipe that could satisfy my cravings. I even experimented with different spices to see what I loved most. This recipe was my favorite variation. Bet you can't have just one bite!

holy guacamole!

By: Alex Jamieson

Ingredients

2 large ripe avocados

2 tsp lime juice

1 Roma tomato, chopped

1 clove garlic, minced

⅛ tsp cayenne powder

¼ tsp chili powder

Dash of salt to taste

Directions

1. Mash avocado with a fork until almost smooth, or until desired consistency.
2. Add the rest of the ingredients and mix until well combined. That's it! Dip and enjoy!

Nutritional Benefits

Guacamole is a fun and easy food to prepare that is nutrient dense. Avocados are a source of B-vitamins, vitamin C, A, and E. They contain about 5 grams of protein per fruit and are a great source of good fat and dietary fiber. Also, when you look at an avocado, it resembles a woman's uterus. That is exactly one of the things it is fabulous for—supporting the woman's reproductive system!

Story

Guacamole is a standard in my house—it fills me up, gives me that creamy texture I crave so that I avoid the pitfalls of dairy products, and helps keep my skin healthy with the great fats. Oh, and my son eats it—BONUS!

baba ganoush

By: Briana Santoro

Ingredients

2 large purple eggplants

1 clove of garlic

2 tbsp tahini

1 tbsp olive oil

½ a lemon, juiced

1 tbsp gluten-free tamari

¼ tsp Celtic sea salt

¼ tsp pepper

1 tsp parsley
(or you can use some fresh parsley)

3 tbsp plain yogurt (I use goat's yogurt)

Directions

1. Preheat oven to 375°F.
2. Pierce each eggplant with a fork 15 times. Place on a baking sheet in the oven for 1 hour. Remove from the oven. When cool, cut off the tops and peel (discard peel but leave seeds). Chop into large chunks and put in a food processor with the S-blade.
3. Add the rest of the ingredients to the food processor and process until smooth.
4. Store in the fridge and serve with veggies or crackers. Also can be used in a sandwich or wrap as a healthy substitute for mayonnaise.

Nutritional Benefits

This is a great source of dietary fiber due to the grilled eggplant. Baba ganoush is a wonderful source of the mineral potassium, which is important in the muscular system, and for regulating nerves and the heartbeat of our body. This also provides calcium, iron, and zinc. Although there is a generous amount of fat in baba ganoush (much like hummus), the sources of fat are olive oil and sesame seeds, which are healthy unsaturated fats.

Story

Since hummus would be on my list of foods to bring with me to a desert island, it tends to be the go-to dip in my house. However, sometimes I'm looking for another dip to add to the party—something to shake things up a little! One day I had a couple of eggplants in my fridge that were screaming out at me to be used. I decided to throw them in the oven, roast them up, and turn them into a delicious baba ganoush. I served it at a party the next day and people kept asking me where I bought it. I figured this recipe was a winner and have been using it ever since.

vegan almond basil pesto

By: Marni Wasserman

Ingredients

2 tbsp torn fresh basil

1 tbsp chopped parsley

1 cup whole almonds, soaked overnight or for 8 hours

½ cup pine nuts

2 tbsp lemon juice

1 garlic clove

¼ cup olive oil (or more) for a creamier consistency

Directions

1. Place all ingredients in food processor and blend until smooth
2. Place in a small bowl and refrigerate
3. Serve and enjoy!

Note

This is a delicious spread to enjoy with raw bread, flatbread, and crackers or served with crunchy raw/steamed veggies, kelp noodles, brown rice pasta, or zucchini noodles!

Nutritional Benefits

This pesto helps provide healthy amounts of vitamin K and chlorophyll, thanks to the basil and parsley. While chlorophyll has loads of benefits, one in particular is its ability to help increase red blood cell count in the body. This is beneficial because our red blood cells carry oxygen. Increasing our ability to carry oxygen through the body leads to more energy and overall better health.

Story

I have always liked my pesto really thick and creamy. When the dairy is taken out, something needs to replace it. I love putting this pesto on zucchini noodles. Makes such great summer pasta!

mamma's italian pesto

By: Ashley Anderson and Mark Guarini

Ingredients

1 ⅓ cups fresh sweet basil leaves (Mamma gets hers fresh from the garden)

2 small garlic cloves

¼ cup pine nuts

1 tsp Celtic sea salt

⅓ cup extra-virgin, cold-pressed olive oil (Mamma buys hers from the local Italian market)

¼ cup freshly grated Parmigiano-Reggiano

3 tbsp freshly grated Pecorino Romano (optional)

Directions

1. Rinse the basil leaves and spin dry.
2. Peel the garlic and place it with the basil, pine nuts, salt, and olive oil in a food processor (or, do it like grandma/Nonna, and chop ingredients with a knife by hand—be sure to take your time and prepare with love).
3. Run the processor until the mixture is smooth and creamy.
4. Transfer the contents to a mixing bowl and mix in the grated cheeses with a spoon or rubber spatula.

Note

One key to perfect pesto is finely chopping all the ingredients by hand (can take up to 20–30 minutes), preferably with a sharp Mezzaluna or knife. Pesto can be made ahead of time and frozen for up to 3 months. After adding the cheeses, place the pesto in an ice cube tray and coat the surface with olive oil before placing in the freezer. Place in a freezer-safe bag for extra freshness, and add to soups, stews… anything, as you wish.

Nutritional Benefits

Sweet basil not only smells wonderful, but it has wonderful effects on the body, namely anti-inflammatory and anti-bacterial. It is also high in antioxidants and helps bring down stress. Garlic, in addition to being an antimicrobial, provides food for probiotics (good bacteria), and helps lower blood pressure. Olive oil is a great source of omega-6 fatty acids and antioxidants. It's important to note that the fresher the olive oil, the more antioxidant properties it contains. To increase omega-3 fatty acids, walnut oil would be a great substitute for olive oil in this recipe.

Makes about ¾ cup

Story

My mom, Nina Guarini, loves to prepare meals and entertain. She loves to see people smile and enjoy her food. Before holistic chefs, there were our grandmothers. Like Nina, their meals are prepared with love and whole foods. Going home for me, I can always expect a healthy and delicious meal that makes me savor every bite! Mamma infuses so much love into her Italian meals that I can truly taste it! It's so nourishing and leaves me feeling great. This is one of Mamma's favorite recipes that she uses often. Like Mamma says, "Mangiare, mangiare!" ("Eat, eat") and enjoy!

avocado pesto

By: Ashley Anderson and Mark Guarini

Ingredients

1 ½ cups fresh basil leaves

1 medium avocado, pitted and peeled

½ cup raw pine nuts

½ cup nutritional yeast

¼ cup extra-virgin cold-pressed olive oil

¼ cup grapeseed oil

3 small cloves garlic

2 tbsp freshly squeezed lemon juice

½ tsp Celtic sea salt

Fresh ground pepper, to taste

Directions

1. Place all ingredients in a food processor and pulse until all ingredients are fully mixed, and to desired consistency.
2. Use to flavor all kinds of dishes. Store in refrigerator for up to 1 week. May freeze up to 2 months. Try storing in ice cube trays in the freezer for quick small portions to add to soups, stews, baking, and casseroles.

Makes about 2 cups

Nutritional Benefits

Nutritional yeast is an excellent vegan source of nerve nourishing vitamin B12. Avocados, one of Mark's favorite fruits, are low in carbohydrates, and super high in fiber and omega fatty acids. Lemon juice supports good digestion and liver detoxification. Pine nuts are a good source of vitamin A, vitamin C, and lutein, all great for supporting healthy vision and a healthy immune system.

Story

I love Mark's Mamma's homemade pesto (recipe on page 61) but feel best when I minimize and skip the dairy. So I set out to create a dairy-free option. Like so many others living with IBD, IBS, and lactose intolerance, I experience many of the same symptoms when I eat dairy: bloating, gas, indigestion, upset tummy, and often alternating constipation and diarrhea. Health for me is always about listening to my body. This avocado pesto recipe is soothing to my digestion, leaving my tummy happy. Mark is such a great supporter that he helped me develop this pesto by being my official 'taste tester'. I'm happy to report that this recipe is Mark and Mamma Nina approved!

duck liver pâté

By: Briana Santoro

Ingredients

1 lb (454 g) organic duck livers (make sure the gallbladder has been removed)

1 onion, diced

2 cloves garlic, crushed

½ cup unsalted butter

One 2 oz (50 g) can of anchovies, finely chopped

½ tsp Celtic sea salt

½ tsp pepper

1 tsp thyme

1 tsp basil

½ tsp coriander

3 tbsp balsamic vinegar

½ cup cashew cream (optional but highly recommended—see note to the right) (recipe on page 47)

Directions

1. In a frying pan on medium heat melt 1 tbsp of the butter. Add in garlic and onion. Stir and cook for 3–5 minutes (don't allow to burn).
2. Add anchovies, salt, pepper, thyme, basil, and coriander. Stir and cook for another 3–5 minutes.
3. Wash liver and chop into small pieces. Add to pan and cook for 10 minutes or until livers are cooked.
4. Add balsamic vinegar and cook for final 3 minutes.
5. Add the mixture from the pan into a food processor and process until smooth.
6. Cut the remaining butter into chunks and add to the food processor. Also add the cashew cream (if using). Process again until smooth.
7. Scoop into a container and serve warm or refrigerate and serve cold.

Makes 2 cups of pâté

Note

If you choose not to add the cashew cream your pâté will be darker and harder when refrigerated. You will need to leave it out to soften slightly before eating.

Nutritional Benefits

The health of this dish depends on the health of the liver you purchase. Make sure you know your butcher and trust their source. You want to look for liver from ducks that have been raised properly without the use of hormones, antibiotics, or commercial feed. Animal products from animals raised properly have significantly more nutrients (e.g. vitamins A, D, E, K2, B12). Organ meat like liver is one of the highest food sources of nutrients. The animals store these nutrients in the organ and when we consume them we benefit from those nutrients in our body.

Story

After I got married my husband and I went to Italy for our honeymoon. While in Florence we did a full-day private cooking course. I was in heaven! One of the recipes we made was chicken liver pâté. I had heard about the health benefits of liver but had never purchased it or cooked with it before. This was new unchartered territory and I was pumped to dive in! When I got back home I was at my local Healthy Butcher and noticed that they sold duck liver. I bought it and set out to create my own holistic duck liver pâté recipe. This is the creation! Every time I serve it my family and friends go on and on about how good it is. So unless they are just humoring me, I would say we have a winner!

scrumptious seed crackers

By: Shannon Kadlovski

Ingredients

- 1½ cups brown rice flour
- 2 tbsp honey
- ½ tsp sea salt
- ½ cup sesame seeds
- ¼ cup ground flaxseed
- ⅓ cup sunflower seeds
- ¼ cup ground pumpkin seeds
- 1 cup water
- 2 tbsp grapeseed oil

HONEY/WATER MIXTURE

- 2 tbsp honey
- 1 tbsp warm water
- sea salt to taste

Directions

1. Preheat oven to 350°F.
2. Line rimmed cookie sheet with parchment paper.
3. Combine all ingredients except water in a bowl.
4. Once combined, add water and stir dough.
5. Knead dough with hands until all ingredients are combined.
6. Place dough on baking sheet and spread evenly using your hands (it helps to place parchment paper over the dough).
7. Make sure dough is spread thin to ensure crispy crackers.
8. Using a pizza cutter, score the dough into squares.
9. Bake for 10–15 minutes and remove from oven.
10. Flip crackers over one at a time, then place back into the oven and bake until deep golden brown (another 10–15 minutes or so). Bake for longer if you want them to be crispier.
11. Remove from oven and brush with honey/water mixture (see below)
12. Store in an airtight container.

HONEY/WATER MIXTURE DIRECTIONS

1. In a small bowl mix together honey and water.
2. Brush mixture onto baked crackers.
3. Once you have brushed this mixture on the crackers, sprinkle a little bit of sea salt on top for seasoning.

Makes roughly 45–55 crackers

Nutritional Benefits

Many crackers on the market contain refined flours, hydrogenated fat, sugar, and additives. These homemade honey seed crackers use brown rice flour, which is much easier to digest than refined flours. It is also a great source of B vitamins, which help increase energy and decrease stress. Pumpkin seeds provide a healthy dose of zinc, and both pumpkin seeds and flaxseeds are rich in omega-3 and omega-6 fats, and fiber.

Story

These crackers are really simple to make and are always a dinner party favorite. I like to serve them with homemade hummus or dip, and they are always the first thing to go when I offer them to my guests. They are great to have as a staple snack at home as well, and they are easy to take on-the-go. They taste great on their own or with a dip. They are fun to make—I like the process of rolling out the dough, cutting them into pieces, and watching them crisp up in the oven.

sweet cucumber rolls

By: Briana Santoro

Ingredients

1 large English cucumber

1 large ripe Hass avocado, pit and skin removed and sliced into 1 cm strips

1 ripe mango, pit and skin removed and sliced into 1 cm strips

20 pecan halves

40 mint leaves

7 strawberries, cut into approximately 1 cm thick slices

1 tbsp balsamic vinegar

½ tbsp honey

Directions

1. Cut the ends off the cucumber and cut the cucumber in half. Using a vegetable peeler create ribbons out of the cucumber. To do this start by making the first peel of the cucumber as if you were going to peel it. However, continue to peel in the exact same spot until you have peeled the whole cucumber into long thin ribbons. If your peeler blade is smaller than the width of the cucumber, simply cut the side off the cucumber and continue. You should get approximately 10 ribbons from each half of the cucumber depending on how wide it is.

2. Lay the cucumber ribbons out on a flat surface. Place 2 mint leaves on top of each ribbon, close to one of the ends. Place 1 strawberry slice, 1 mango slice, 1 avocado slice, and 1 pecan on top. Carefully roll up the cucumber around the filling. Place upright on a serving dish.

3. To make the dip, mix the balsamic vinegar and honey together, and place in a bowl. Serve the cucumber rolls with the dip and enjoy!

Note

You will be left with some of the mango and avocado, as this recipe does not use an entire avocado or mango. This makes a great salad topper!

Makes approximately 20 rolls

Nutritional Benefits

This is a great raw appetizer full of digestive enzymes, healthy fats, phytonutrients, and vitamin C.

Story

The combination of flavors in this appetizer will result in fireworks going off in your mouth! These little rolls are fun to make and they look like a gourmet masterpiece when they are done. Trust me when I say they will be the talk of the party. The only problem is that they are so good they often don't make it as far as the party!

coconut mussels

By: Briana Santoro

Ingredients

2 lbs (907 g) mussels

1 tbsp coconut oil

1 onion, diced

2 cloves of garlic, finely chopped

1 chili pepper, finely chopped or ⅛ tsp of cayenne pepper

3 Roma tomatoes, diced

1 can of coconut milk

Directions

1. Add coconut oil to a large pot on medium heat and melt. Add onion and garlic to the pot and sauté for 3 minutes (do not burn).
2. Add tomatoes and chili pepper (or cayenne) to the pot. Cover and cook for 10 minutes.
3. Add coconut milk, stir, turn up the heat to medium-high, and boil for 15 minutes uncovered. Stir frequently.
4. Rinse and scrub the mussels under cold water. Throw away any mussels that have already opened up wide, as they are already dead.
5. Add the mussels to the pot, stir, cover, and cook on medium heat for another 5 minutes or until the mussels open up wide. Serve hot and enjoy!

Serves 4-6

Nutritional Benefits

Mussels are a great source of lean protein. They also have more omega-3 fatty acids than other shellfish, which makes them helpful for fighting inflammation. They pack a punch when it comes to nutrients and are high in iron, selenium, zinc, and vitamin B12 (helpful for energy).

Story

What I love about serving mussels at a dinner party is that it turns eating food into a fun activity. I'm all about trying to bring people closer to our food and I find mussels definitely help to achieve this. When serving mussels I give each guest an empty bowl and then put a massive bowl in the middle of the table piled high with the yummy cooked mussels, so guests can serve themselves. We dive in using a fork to pull out the mussel and we use one of the half shells to scoop it up for eating, making sure to also scoop up the creamy coconut sauce. Guests then toss their empty shells in a big empty bowl on the table. Just picture it, everyone sharing one big communal dish, empty mussel shells flying around, using mussel shells as a serving utensil, laughter, smiles, and enjoyment. So much fun!!

Spunky Baked Chicken Meatballs

By: Connie Jeon

Ingredients

1 cup organic zucchini, chopped (about 1 zucchini)

1 cup organic carrots, chopped (about 2 carrots)

½ cup parsley, coarsely chopped

3 medium cloves garlic

¼ cup blanched almond flour

1 organic egg

1 lb (454 g) boneless skinless organic chicken breasts, cut into chunks

1 tsp sea salt

½ tsp ground pepper

¼ tsp chili powder

Directions

1. Preheat oven to 350°F.
2. In a food processor, pulse together the zucchini, carrots, parsley, and garlic.
3. Add almond flour, egg, chicken, salt, pepper, and chili powder and process until thoroughly combined.
4. Drop tablespoon sized balls of the chicken mixture onto a parchment lined baking sheet.
5. Bake meatballs for 20 to 25 minutes or until fully cooked through. Serve!

Makes 15–20 meatballs
(Depending on the size of the balls)

Nutritional Benefits

The almond flour is a great substitute for the traditional flour used in meatballs. This is because almond flour is gluten-free, wheat-free, and tends to be more easily digested. Also, using chicken breasts provides a leaner form of protein in comparison to many other meatball recipes.

Story

These meatballs are a timeless favorite in my household. My boys help me gauge how delicious my recipes taste. If I can get these picky eaters to savor all the goodness of the real food, then I've done my job. I like making these because I can save some for pasta dishes as well. Hope you enjoy them!

sexy rice nut rolls

By: Melissa Ramos

Ingredients

2 cups walnuts

1 cup sunflower seeds

2 cloves garlic, minced

½ tsp cumin

2 tbsp tamari

2 tbsp apple cider vinegar

Pinch of sea salt and cracked pepper (or as needed)

2 large kale leaves with the stem cut out for ease of rolling

2 carrots, shredded

Several rice paper wraps (approximately 6)

Directions

1. Grind walnuts and sunflower seeds together into a crumbly powder using a food processor or high-speed blender. Add garlic, cumin, tamari, apple cider vinegar, salt and pepper. Process until well combined.

2. Add water if needed to make sure the mixture isn't crumbly.

3. Put rice paper wraps in a bowl of warm water until pliable. Lay the wrap out flat and top with kale (about ⅓ of one leaf), some nut mixture, and some shredded carrot. Fold over ¼ of both sides of the wrap and then roll up the wrap from the bottom. Repeat until the nut mixture is used up.

Serves 4-6

Note:

These rolls go great with the Sunflower Seed Dip on page 69.

Nutritional Benefits

From a nutritional perspective, this is a great veggie snack that's light and completely satisfying. The healthy fats and carbs that these wraps contain are incredible for a light pick-me-up that will help to keep you full without the sugar crash of many commercial snacks.

Story

These make me so happy. They're so meaty inside yet fresh tasting on the outside. Therefore, you get the best of both worlds. I remember making this for my partner and to my dismay my snacks for lunch the next day were devoured. So my caution to you is: be careful whom you share these with, because they'll likely get taken away from you!

sunflower seed dip

By: Briana Santoro

Ingredients

½ cup sunflower seed butter

3 tbsp lemon juice

1 tbsp gluten-free tamari

½–1 tbsp honey, depending on how sweet you want it

¼ cup water

1 clove garlic, minced

Directions

1. Mix all the ingredients together in a bowl until well combined.

Note

This dip goes great with vegetables and fruit (e.g. celery/carrot sticks or apple/pear slices). Kids love it! It is also great as a dipping sauce for the Sexy Rice Nut Rolls found on page 68.

Makes just over 1 cup of dip

Nutritional Benefits

Sunflower seed butter is a great alternative to peanut butter for people who are allergic to nuts. Also, if you work with someone or go to school with someone who has a nut allergy, opting for sunflower seed butter is a great alternative. This is especially true because nut allergies tend to be very serious and even very minor exposure (e.g. breathing on someone after eating peanut butter) can cause an anaphylactic reaction. Sunflower seed butter is also a great source of protein and vitamin E, which is the body's primary fat-soluble antioxidant.

Story

There is a sweet spot in my heart for cold rice paper rolls, like the type you see in Thai restaurants. I love making them myself and filling them with different veggies, sprouts, chicken, etc. When my good friend Melissa Ramos created the Sexy Rice Nut Rolls recipe (found on page 68), I was in heaven! The nut filling is absolutely delicious! One day when I was eating them I decided to experiment and create a dipping sauce. The sauce they serve with rolls at restaurants may taste delicious but is usually full of processed sugar and other potentially harmful ingredients. I wanted to create a sauce that was delicious but also healthy. This is what I came up with. In my opinion, we have a winner!

butter chicken wraps

By: Briana Santoro

MAKING THE CHICKEN

Ingredients

2 chicken breasts

½ tbsp olive oil

Juice of half a lime

3 pinches of Celtic sea salt and pepper

½ tbsp fresh grated ginger

Directions

1. Preheat oven to 300°F.
2. Put all ingredients in a bowl, stir, cover the bowl, and let marinate for 1 hour or more.
3. Bake chicken with the marinading liquid in a covered baking dish for 40 minutes or until cooked. Cut the chicken into chunks and set aside.

Nutritional Benefits

This recipe is filled with amazing aromatic herbs and spices that are very warming to the body and great for digestion. This includes cayenne, cumin, coriander, turmeric, ginger, and garlic. In particular, turmeric purifies and nourishes the blood and is very balancing to all of the Ayurvedic doshas.

MAKING THE BUTTER CHICKEN

Ingredients

2 tbsp butter

2 cloves garlic, crushed

1 onion, diced

1 tbsp ginger

¼ tsp cayenne

1 ½ tsp each of turmeric, cumin, and coriander

½ tsp each of cinnamon and Celtic sea salt

⅛ tsp pepper

4 Roma tomatoes

2 tbsp honey

1 cup plain goat's yogurt OR 1 cup cashew cream (recipe on page 47)

1 head of Boston lettuce, leaves removed, washed, and dried

3 green onions, chopped including the greens (for garnish)

Cilantro chopped (for garnish)

Slivered or shaved almonds (for garnish)

Story

I LOVE this recipe! Years ago when I completed my undergraduate degree, my husband Steve and I moved to South Korea for a year to teach. We then travelled around the world for 4 months. We spent a month in India and India became one of my favorite countries. One of the reasons for this was the food! The combination of spices and the flavors they use are incredibly delicious! I'm a big fan of butter chicken but often find that recipes for this dish are not very healthy. In addition, the store bought sauces I've seen are a big no-no as they are full of unhealthy ingredients. This recipe combines health with flavor and will have you coming back for more!

Directions

1. Melt butter in a pan on medium heat. Add garlic and onion. Sauté until translucent (approximately 7–10 min).
2. Add all the spices and stir.
3. Cut tomatoes into chunks and blend in a high-speed blender until there are no more big chunks. Pour tomatoes into pan and add honey. Stir and cook for another 20 minutes.
4. Add chopped chicken and yogurt/cashew cream. Turn to low and stir until warm.
5. Put lettuce leaves on a plate and top with 1–2 tbsp of butter chicken. Garnish with slivered/shaved almonds, green onion, and cilantro.

Note

This can also be served as a meal for lunch or dinner.

Makes 16–18 small wraps

sour cream and onion kale chips

By: Briana Santoro

Ingredients

1 ½ heads organic kale (recommended) or 1 large conventional head of kale

2 tbsp extra-virgin cold-pressed olive oil

2 tbsp tahini

½ tbsp Bragg's Liquid Aminos or tamari

¼ tsp Celtic sea salt

3 green onions, chopped finely

1 tbsp apple cider vinegar

Directions

1. Wash and dry kale (it's important that the kale is dry). Remove spine of kale and break up the leafy part into smaller pieces. Put in a bowl.

2. Put the remaining ingredients into a blender or small food processor and blend for a few seconds until creamy, or place ingredients in a jar and shake until the ingredients are all mixed together.

3. Pour the sauce over the kale and using your hands mix in the sauce so the kale is well coated.

4. Spread kale out on dehydrator trays and dehydrate at 110°F for approximately 8 hours or until dry.

Note

This recipe works best in a dehydrator. If you don't have a dehydrator you could make the chips in the oven by baking them on a broiler pan at 350°F for 13 minutes. If you do this it's important to make sure the kale leaves are laying flat on the pan and do not overlap. For better results using the oven to make kale chips, don't use the sauce listed in this recipe. Just sprinkle a little bit of olive oil and sea salt on the kale leaves and bake.

Nutritional Benefits

Kale is one of those wondrous superfoods. It's a dark leafy green that is filled with an abundance of vitamins and minerals including calcium and magnesium. Both of these minerals work hand in hand in the body. For example, calcium helps to contract the heart muscle and magnesium helps to relax it.

Story

Talk about love at first bite! Kale chips are like a gift from the health food gods. When you eat them, you have to keep wondering, "how can healthy food taste this freakin' good"! Once I fell in love with them, I started to experiment with different flavors. This sour cream and onion recipe was the favorite in my house. I can tell because it is always the batch that disappears the fastest! If they make it 24 hours, I'm shocked.

cauliflower popcorn

By: Julie Daniluk

Excerpted from Meals That Heal Inflammation: Embrace Healthy Living and Eliminate Pain, One Meal at a Time by Julie Daniluk. Copyright © 2011 Daniluk Consulting. Reprinted by permission of Random House Canada and Hay House, Inc.

Ingredients

4 cups cauliflower (1 large head)

2 tbsp extra-virgin olive oil

Grey sea salt or pink rock salt to taste

1 tbsp nutritional yeast

Directions

1. Preheat oven to 350°F.
2. Trim the head of cauliflower, discarding the core and thick stems. Cut florets into pieces about the size of Ping-Pong balls.
3. In a large bowl, whisk together the olive oil and salt, then add the cauliflower pieces and toss thoroughly.
4. Line a baking sheet with unbleached parchment, if you have it, for easy cleanup, then spread the cauliflower pieces on the sheet and sprinkle evenly with nutritional yeast.
5. Roast for 1 hour, turning 3 or 4 times, until most of each piece has turned golden brown.

Makes 4 cups

Nutritional Benefits

Nutritional yeast is not a live yeast and therefore does not throw off the delicate digestive balance of the gut in the same way that live brewer's yeast (found in alcohol) does. It is one of nature's richest sources of B vitamins, providing energy and nourishment to the nervous system. Nutritional yeast is available in many health food stores and grocery stores with health-food sections.

Story

The idea of cauliflower popcorn was inspired by the crispy brown edges and buttery taste of the cauliflower in this simple dish.

apple jar

By: Alicia Diaz

Ingredients

1 large sweet apple

¼ cup water

1 handful of currants or raisins

1 tsp cinnamon

½ tsp cardamom

½ tbsp fresh grated ginger

Directions

1. Chop apple, leaving the skin on, and toss with all ingredients in a small saucepan on medium heat.
2. Let apple stew in spices just until soft (about 5 minutes).

Serves 1

Nutritional Benefits

Stewed apples are considered in Ayurveda to be extremely balancing to the colon. Almost every one of my clients that are experiencing low energy and fatigue have some kind of imbalance in their digestion, particularly the colon. Also, the added iron in the raisins and currants helps to build blood, which can also boost energy!

Story

This sweet and wholesome little apple jar has been a dear companion of mine on days I know I'm going to be out 'n' about and might need a little mid-morning or mid-afternoon snack. It's easy to digest and the warm spices are reminiscent of a relaxing autumn day.

fruit kabobs rolled in trail mix

By: Alex Jamieson

Ingredients

2 bananas
8 strawberries
¼ cup sesame seeds
¼ cup pumpkin seeds
¼ cup raisins
½ cup unsweetened shredded coconut
Dairy-free yogurt

Directions

1. Cut 2 bananas into 4 pieces each.
2. Wash, dry, and de-stem the strawberries.
3. Mix all the seeds, raisins, and coconut together in a bowl.
4. Skewer pieces of banana and washed strawberries on toothpicks or popsicle sticks.
5. Dip fruit skewers gently in a bowl filled with dairy-free yogurt and roll them in the trail mix.

Serves 2

Nutritional Benefits

When you are craving a sweet treat it can sometimes be difficult to make a healthy decision. Using fruit to satisfy your sweet tooth is a wise choice and these fruit kabobs are a tasty and healthy treat. Bananas are rich in fiber, potassium, and are sweeter as they become ripe. Sesame seeds and pumpkin seeds are an easy way to consume healthy fats, minerals, and plant protein.

Story

I first started making this in my cooking-with-kids classes—you know, just trying to help little hands learn how to play with healthy foods. Then I started eating them on a regular basis myself—I guess I never grew up!

chocolate chickpea power bars

By: Shannon Kadlovski

Ingredients

One 14 oz (398 ml) can of chickpeas (BPA-free can)

½ cup sunflower seed butter (you can use natural nut/seed butter of your choice)

¾ cup pure maple syrup

1 banana, mashed

1 tsp pure vanilla extract

¼ tsp sea salt

1 ½ cups rolled oats

½ cup cacao (or carob) powder

½ cup 100% New Zealand whey or vegan protein powder

¾ cup unsweetened shredded coconut

¼ cup dried cranberries

¼ tsp matcha green tea powder

1 tsp grapeseed oil

Directions

1. Preheat oven to 350°F.
2. Rinse chickpeas with water and strain.
3. In a food processor combine chickpeas, seed butter, maple syrup, banana, vanilla extract, and salt until smooth.
4. Add the oats, cacao powder, and protein powder. Pulse just to combine.
5. Add coconut, cranberries, and matcha powder. Pulse again just to combine.
6. Grease a 9" x 9" square pan with grapeseed oil and spread mixture into pan.
7. Bake in the oven for 18–20 minutes.
8. Cut into bars or squares right away and let cool in pan.
9. Once cooled, remove from pan and serve!

Makes 12–15 bars

Nutritional Benefits

These power bars are jam-packed with fiber and protein! This comes from the chickpeas, seed butter, rolled oats, and protein powder. Boosting our fiber consumption helps keep our digestive system smiling and working optimally. In addition, consuming appropriate amounts of protein is important because it is an essential building block for muscles, bones, cartilage, skin, and blood.

Story

These chickpea power bars are perfect for an afternoon energy boost or for breakfast on-the-go. I like to make a big batch every couple of weeks and I always keep a bar with me for those "stuck in traffic and starving" moments. They keep really well in the fridge or freezer and are always a huge hit when I bring them to dinner parties—even the kids love them!

apple pie "ice cream" (great for kids!)

By: Alex Jamieson

Ingredients

8 Medjool dates, pitted

3–4 Honeycrisp apples, cored

½ cup oat bran

½ tsp ground cinnamon

Directions

1. Have the kids use plastic or kid-safe knives to remove the date pits and throw them away.
2. Cut the apples into quarters and remove the seeds and core. Use the grating/shredding blade in your food processor to grate the apples. Scoop into a large mixing bowl.
3. Replace the grating/shredding blade with the S-blade and combine the apples, dates, oat bran, and cinnamon together. Pulse until the ingredients are well combined.
4. Scoop the "ice cream" into the mixing bowl and use an ice cream scooper to give each person a share.

Serves 4–6

Nutritional Benefits

With all the oat bran and apples, this recipe will add a nice dose of fiber for those constipation-inclined readers! Also, oat bran is high in a type of fiber called soluble fiber, which is known to lower LDL cholesterol. More importantly, studies have shown that a diet high in soluble fiber may lower the risk of getting heart disease.

Story

Anything becomes "ice cream" when scooped with an ice cream scooper. I believe everything instantly becomes 77% more fun when served in the shape of a scoop of ice cream. 'Nuff said.

ginger appetizer

By: Alicia Diaz

Ingredients

4 small spoons

4 thin slices of peeled fresh ginger

1 pinch Himalayan salt or Celtic sea salt

1 wedge of lime or lemon

1 tsp raw honey

Directions

1. Place one slice of ginger on top of each spoon.
2. Top each slice of ginger with a pinch of salt, squeeze of lime/lemon, and dollop of raw honey. Serve and enjoy!

Serves 4

Nutritional Benefits

Raw ginger combined with the other ingredients encourages natural stomach enzymes to be released. This in turn helps you become more energized after you eat a meal, rather than feeling sluggish or sleepy.

Story

This light and invigorating appetizer will do wonders for the amount of nutrients you are able to absorb from your meal! This is another simple treat that I used to heal my digestion and to help many of my clients as well. It's spicy and tangy but has a smooth sweetness from the raw honey.

salads

SPINACH, STRAWBERRY, AND CANDIED PECAN SALAD	80
RUBY GRAPEFRUIT, AVOCADO, AND FENNEL SALAD	81
EDAMAME AND AVOCADO SALAD	82
NAPA CABBAGE SALAD	83
SWEET POTATO SALAD	84
CRISPY CHICKPEA KALE SALAD	85
MEDITERRANEAN QUINOA SALAD	86
ROAST VEGETABLE SALAD WITH YOGURT DRESSING	87
RAW SWEET POTATO NOODLE SALAD	88
FRESH AND COOL QUINOA SALAD	89
'WILDLY' FABULOUS SEAFOOD SALAD	90
APPLE, ARUGULA, AND CHICKEN SALAD	91
LEAFY WALDORF SALAD	92
WATERMELON SALAD	93
KALE SLAW SALAD	94
AVOCADO CHICKEN CAESAR SALAD	95

spinach, strawberry, and candied pecan salad

By: Briana Santoro

Ingredients

4 cups baby spinach

5 strawberries, sliced

¼ large Haas avocado, pit and skin removed and sliced

3 tbsp crumbled goat cheese

½ cup pecans

1 tbsp + 2 tsp maple syrup

1 ½ tbsp olive oil

1 ½ tbsp balsamic vinegar

2 pinches Celtic sea salt and pepper

Directions

1. In a salad bowl put spinach, strawberries, avocado, and goat cheese.

2. Put pecans in a frying pan and toast them on medium heat, stirring frequently until lightly toasted. Add 1 tbsp maple syrup and stir until pecans are coated. Remove from heat and spread the pecans out evenly in the frying pan. Allow them to cool for 5 minutes and then add to salad.

Note

If you let the pecans cool for longer they may stick to the pan. If you make them ahead of time, transfer them to a glass container after 5 minutes of cooling and store in the fridge.

3. In a small bowl or jar mix olive oil, balsamic vinegar, 2 tsp maple syrup, salt, and pepper until well combined. Add the dressing to the salad, toss, and enjoy!

Serves 2

Nutritional Benefits

If there were a competition for the world's healthiest foods—spinach would be a nominee. It is loaded in vitamins (like vitamin K), minerals (like magnesium), and phytonutrients (like beta-carotene). Most people are deficient in magnesium these days, so consuming spinach and other leafy greens will help to boost our magnesium levels and help avoid deficiency.

Story

Anyone who thinks salads are boring or not full of flavor must not have tried this one! This salad tastes so incredible you will feel like you should be eating it for dessert! Whenever I make this salad I make it nice and big. I often wonder if I've made too much. However, to this day there has never been any salad leftover. It always goes, leaves people licking their lips and wishing they could turn back time so they can experience those delicious tastes one more time!

ruby grapefruit, avocado, and fennel salad

By: James Colquhoun and Laurentine ten Bosch

From The Food Matters Recipe Book www.FoodMatters.tv

Ingredients

2 ruby (pink) grapefruits

2 avocados, pit and skin removed and sliced

1 large or 2 small fennel bulbs

1 small handful of mint leaves, torn

1 tbsp lime juice

2 tbsp cold-pressed, extra-virgin olive or macadamia nut oil

Unrefined sea salt

Freshly ground pepper

Directions

1. Cut the thick peel and pith from the top and bottom of the grapefruit, then stand upright on your chopping board. Using a mandolin or carefully with a sharp knife slice thin slices downward on all sides to remove the peel, white pith, and expose the pink flesh. Hold the grapefruit in your hand and carefully cut segments out from between the membranes. Place the segments in a large bowl or on a platter.
2. Squeeze any residual juice from the remaining core into a separate bowl.
3. Add the avocado slices, fennel, and mint to the grapefruit segments.
4. In a glass jar put the oil, lime juice, 1 tbsp of the remaining grapefruit juice, a generous pinch of salt, and ground pepper and shake. Pour dressing over the salad and toss gently.

Serves 2–3

Note

If you can't get ruby red grapefruit, oranges work well also.

Nutritional Benefits

Avocados are a great non-sweet fruit and an excellent source of healthy monounsaturated fats, protective vitamin E, and dietary fiber. Like tomatoes, ruby grapefruits are high in heart healthy lycopene. They are refreshing and bursting with health properties that support our liver, keeping it healthy and ensuring our natural detoxification pathways are in tip-top shape.

Story

This is a cleansing and refreshing salad. We love having it on a hot summer's day. We also find that it is a delicious accompaniment to fish!

edamame and avocado salad

By: Shannon Kadlovski

Ingredients

3 cups organic shelled edamame

1 avocado, pit and skin removed and chunked

1 green onion, chopped

⅓ cup parsley, finely chopped

2 large stalks of kale, finely chopped with spine removed

DRESSING

1 tbsp olive oil

2 tbsp apple cider vinegar

1 clove garlic, crushed

¼ tsp sea salt

Pepper to taste

Juice of 1 lime

Directions

1. Boil frozen shelled edamame for 4 minutes.
2. Remove from heat and rinse with cold water.
3. Place edamame into a medium size bowl.
4. Chop parsley, green onion, kale, and avocado and add to edamame.
5. In a small bowl, combine all ingredients for dressing.
6. Mix dressing ingredients in a bowl or jar. Pour dressing on top of edamame salad.
7. Refrigerate until ready to serve.

Makes 4 small servings

Nutritional Benefits

The edamame used in this delicious salad is a good source of vegetarian protein, fiber, and phytoestrogens. Avocado lends a creamy texture and is rich in monounsaturated "healthy" fat. Kale is a super-green full of vitamins and vital minerals that help our body achieve a balanced pH level, while detoxing harmful chemicals.

Story

Avocado is one of my favorite foods, and I always like to toss it into a salad, add it to a sandwich, or have it with some eggs. The edamame and avocado combination is great because you get the crunchy texture from the beans and the creamy texture from the avocado—I like the different textures together. This salad is also one of the quickest and easiest salads to make, so it's always a good option for those extra busy days.

Napa Cabbage Salad

By: Marni Wasserman

Ingredients

1 whole Napa cabbage, washed and sliced into shreds

¼ cup soaked arame

1 cup shelled cooked organic edamame (optional)

⅓ cup sunflower seeds, toasted

2 tbsp sesame seeds or poppy seeds

DRESSING

⅓ cup olive oil

¼ cup brown rice syrup

¼ cup brown rice vinegar

1 tbsp tamari

1 tbsp sesame oil

1 small or medium onion, grated

1–2 cloves garlic, minced

Directions

1. Soak arame in water for 20 minutes.
2. Place the cabbage in a large salad bowl with the edamame. Add in soaked arame. In a smaller bowl, combine all the ingredients for the dressing and mix well.
3. Pour over the salad mixture in the bowl, then top with the seeds and toss. Serve immediately.

Serves 6–8

Nutritional Benefits

Grown in the depths of the sea, seaweed is full of vitamins and minerals essential to human health and nutritional balance. The most significant minerals found in sea greens are calcium, iodine, phosphorous, sodium, and iron. One of the many things sea vegetables can help with is removing metallic and radioactive elements from the body. Plus, we can't forget about the Napa cabbage, which is a great source of folate, an important nutrient for expectant mothers.

Story

This recipe was first created for my Asian themed cooking class. I wanted a light crispy salad that used all my favorite Asian condiments and as such, this salad was made.

sweet potato salad

By: Shannon Kadlovski

Ingredients

2 medium sweet potatoes, peeled and cubed

1 medium red onion, cut into small pieces

¼ cup dried cranberries or raisins

Handful of chopped parsley

1 tbsp olive oil

Pinch of sea salt and ground pepper

DRESSING

2 tbsp olive oil

2 tsp Dijon mustard

1 tsp raw honey or pure maple syrup

¼ tsp sea salt

Pinch of black pepper

Directions

1. Preheat oven to 400°F.
2. Place potatoes and onions in a bowl with olive oil, salt, and pepper.
3. Place onto baking sheet lined with parchment paper or glass baking dish, and bake for 30 minutes or until tender.
4. Combine dressing ingredients into a small bowl.
5. Once potatoes are roasted, remove from oven, let cool, and then add to a salad bowl.
6. Top with cranberries/raisins and parsley.
7. Pour dressing on top and stir.
8. Place in the fridge and serve cold, or serve immediately if you want it to be a warm salad.

Serves 4–5 as a side salad

Nutritional Benefits

This salad is a nice alternative to the traditional creamy potato salads that can be made with loads of saturated fat. Sweet potatoes contain the antioxidants beta-carotene and vitamin C, important for collagen production and healthy eyes. Sweet potatoes are also a great source of fiber and complex carbohydrates, which help to improve digestion and provide energy. Parsley helps to detoxify the body and is also rich in vitamin K.

Story

Sweet potatoes are the perfect side dish to any meal. I like them because they are sweet and don't require heavy sauces and added flavors to make them taste delicious. They are filling but not in a way that makes you feel bloated or tired after eating them. They actually provide that slow burning energy, and do not result in the same energy crash that other carbohydrate-rich foods do. I like a salad that speaks for itself just based on its ingredients, rather than having the dressing as the feature flavor. Even without dressing, this dish is one of my favorites.

Crispy Chickpea Kale Salad

By: Jesse Schelew

Ingredients

1 can chickpeas, drained and patted dry
3 tbsp sesame seeds
3 tbsp sunflower seeds
3 tbsp pumpkin seeds
3 tbsp coconut oil, melted
1 tsp cumin
1 tsp garlic powder
½ tsp coriander
½ tsp pepper
½ tsp paprika
¼ tsp turmeric
¼ tsp cayenne pepper
1 head kale, stems removed and chopped/torn into bite-size pieces
2 avocados, pits and skin removed and sliced or chunked

DRESSING

¾ cup raw cashews
2 garlic cloves
¾ cup tahini
2 tsp miso paste
1 tsp apple cider vinegar
Juice of ¼ a lemon (1 tbsp)
2 tsp nutritional yeast
3 tbsp coconut oil, melted
½ cup water
2 tsp tamari
1 tsp pepper

Directions

1. Preheat oven to 400°F and line a baking sheet with parchment paper or a Silpat.
2. In a large bowl mix the chickpeas, sesame seeds, sunflower seeds, pumpkin seeds, 3 tbsp melted coconut oil, cumin, garlic powder, coriander, pepper, paprika, turmeric, and cayenne pepper. Spread out on the baking sheet and cook for 30–40 minutes, stirring every 10 minutes.
3. To make the dressing, place the cashews and garlic in a food processor and pulse until minced. Add the remaining dressing ingredients and blend until smooth. The dressing will be much thicker than regular salad dressing.
4. In a large bowl massage dressing into the kale. Top with the avocado and sprinkle with the roasted chickpea and seed mixture.

Makes 4 large salads

Nutritional Benefits

This salad is bursting with nutrition, and will surely leave you satisfied and energized. Avocados are a nutrient dense fruit high in potassium, magnesium, iron, manganese, most B-vitamins, as well as vitamin C, A, and E. Pumpkin seeds are high in zinc and are also helpful at getting rid of intestinal worms. Kale adds a great texture to any salad and is also another nutrient dense food. For those vegetarians out there, you certainly don't have to worry about protein intake with this balanced meal.

Story

Kale is quickly growing in popularity. This is exciting news for me since I am a huge kale lover! However, there are still a few skeptics out there and people who are not too sure about this green leafy friend. The thing I love about this recipe is that it is so good it has turned every kale skeptic I know into a huge kale lover! Give it a try and see how addictive this delicious creamy and nutritious salad really is.

mediterranean quinoa salad

By: Jesse Schelew

Ingredients

1 red pepper or 1 cup chopped pre-roasted red pepper

1 cup uncooked quinoa

2 tsp extra-virgin olive oil

Juice of one lime

1 tsp ground cumin

Salt and pepper to taste

½ cup chopped cilantro

3 green onions, chopped

1 tbsp chia seeds

1 cup goat feta cheese, drained and diced

Directions

1. Pre-heat oven to 400°F.
2. Cook quinoa as directed on the package and then place in the fridge to cool for 20 minutes.
3. Wash red peppers and place whole in the oven for 20 minutes, turning every 5 minutes until the skin is dark in color. Remove from the oven, cover with paper towel and let sit for 10 minutes. Peel the roasted pepper, discard the seeds, and dice.
4. Meanwhile, whisk together the olive oil, lime juice, cumin, salt, and pepper in a large bowl.
5. Add the cilantro, green onions, chia seeds, feta, roasted red pepper, and quinoa and toss until mixed.

Makes 4 side salads

Nutritional Benefits

Cilantro has the ability to gently detoxify the body of heavy metals. It also has a very refreshing and unique taste. Quinoa is a great alternative for those avoiding wheat or gluten, with the added bonus of containing good amounts of protein. Chia seeds are a great brain food, energizing, and can stabilize blood sugar. It is no wonder that the Aztecs depended on chia seeds as a source of energy. What more could you want out of a salad?

Story

Ever wonder why people living in the Mediterranean look so healthy? Maybe it's the amazing weather or the beautiful scenery, but I think the secret is in the diet! Studies have actually shown that the Mediterranean diet plays a key role in reducing the risk of heart disease and metabolic syndrome. I created this Mediterranean salad for those of us who are not lucky enough to live in the Mediterranean but want to pretend every now and then. This is a refreshing salad with tangy Mediterranean flavors that will transport you to the coast.

roast vegetable salad with yogurt dressing

By: James Colquhoun and Laurentine ten Bosch

From The Food Matters Recipe Book www.FoodMatters.tv

Ingredients

4 handfuls of mixed tender leafy greens

1 handful of fresh herbs (mint, cilantro, or flat leaf parsley), roughly chopped

14 oz (400 g) of pumpkin or butternut squash, peeled and roughly chopped in ½ inch cubes

1 fresh beet, roughly chopped into ½ inch cubes

2 small brown onions, peeled and quartered

1 zucchini, chopped into 1 inch pieces

2 tbsp coconut oil

½ tsp unrefined sea salt

½ tsp cumin powder

½ tsp cinnamon powder

¼ tsp turmeric powder

DRESSING

½ cup natural whole yogurt

Juice of ½ a large lemon

1 tbsp cold-pressed, extra-virgin olive oil

½ clove of garlic, crushed

Unrefined sea salt

Freshly cracked pepper to taste

Directions

1. Preheat your oven to 340°F. If your coconut oil is solid, scoop it onto your baking dish and put this in the oven to melt for a minute first.
2. Add pumpkin, beet, onion, and zucchini to the melted coconut oil, toss to coat and sprinkle with salt and spices. Return to the oven to roast for 45 minutes or until vegetables are golden and softened to your liking. Halfway through cooking, toss vegetables once so they cook evenly.
3. While the vegetables are cooking, stir up the dressing ingredients in a jar or mix in a small bowl. In the large dish, arrange your greens and herbs.
4. When the vegetables are ready, remove from the oven and let them cool slightly, then toss them together with the greens. Serve with the yogurt dressing poured over the top.

Serves 2–4

Note

Try this dish with whatever root vegetables you have access to, including sweet potato or parsnips. For a low starch option (if you're dealing with blood-sugar or weight issues), omit the pumpkin and beetroot and stick to vegetables like zucchini, onion, asparagus, and cauliflower. These all roast up beautifully.

Nutritional Benefits

Fresh herbs (mint, cilantro, and parsley) add a refreshing boost of flavor that also provides a boost of antioxidant power and supports healthy removal of heavy metals from the body. Beets shine bright red telling you they're loaded with health benefits, such as protecting against heart disease, cancer, and high blood pressure.

Story

We love this salad! It's hearty and very tasty. This dish makes a great warming alternative throughout the winter months.

raw sweet potato noodle salad

By: Briana Santoro

Ingredients

3 small or 2 large sweet potatoes

2 heads of broccoli, cut into small pieces and lightly steamed for approximately 2 minutes

5 oz (142 g) grape tomatoes, cut in quarters

15 olives (your favorite type), cut into slices

½ a 7 oz (210 ml) jar of sliced sundried tomatoes, rinsed and strained

¼ cup sesame seeds

1 loose cup of fresh basil

½ cup hemp seeds

½ cup olive oil

2 tbsp nutritional yeast

2 cloves garlic, sliced

1 tbsp + 1 tsp Celtic sea salt

Crumbled goat cheese for garnish (optional)

Directions

1. Turn sweet potatoes into noodles using a spiralizer.
2. Put 1 tbsp of salt on sweet potato noodles in a bowl and let sit for 20 minutes. Rinse and strain out excess water and then put the noodles back in the bowl.
3. In a high-speed blender add basil, hemp hearts, olive oil, nutritional yeast, garlic, and 1 tsp of salt. Blend on medium-low speed until well mixed. It should be the consistency of pesto.
4. Pour pesto on sweet potato noodles and mix in thoroughly with hands (don't be afraid to get a bit messy!).
5. Add broccoli, tomatoes, olives, sundried tomatoes, and sesame seeds. Mix in thoroughly.
6. Keep in fridge until ready to eat. Top with crumbled goat cheese (optional) when serving. Enjoy!

Serves 6

Nutritional Highlights

Sweet potatoes are a great source of fiber, low on the glycemic index, and filled with phytonutrients. Adding a variation of seeds like hemp seeds and sesame seeds are not only great for flavor, but also supply our body with a healthy source of protein and fat.

Story

In my neighborhood there is this amazing healthy restaurant that I love visiting. One time when I was there I noticed they had a raw sweet potato noodle salad. Truthfully I had never eaten sweet potato raw before and was very intrigued by this idea! After eating this salad I fell in love. The noodles have a soft crunchy texture that is amazing. I set out to create a recipe for a similar salad because I loved it so much. The best part about this salad is that it keeps in the fridge for a few days so you can eat it for lunch throughout the week.

fresh and cool quinoa salad

By: Alicia Diaz

Ingredients

1 cup quinoa, rinsed

3 cups water

2 cups diced cucumber

1 avocado, pit and skin removed and cubed

1 cup chopped cilantro

Juice of 1 lime

3 tbsp extra-virgin olive oil

1 small bunch of green onions, finely chopped (optional)

Rock salt and fresh ground pepper to taste

Directions

1. Combine quinoa and water in a pot with the lid on. Bring it to a boil, reduce heat, and simmer for about 15–20 minutes, until cooked and fluffy.

2. After quinoa has cooled, mix all ingredients together in a bowl, leaving aside a bit of avocado and cilantro to use as a garnish for the dish. Enjoy!

Serves 6

Nutritional Benefits

This recipe is very cooling and balancing to individuals who tend to experience a lot of heat, acidity, and inflammation in the body, as well as a tendency towards bouts of anger and frustration. It's also wonderful for all body types to enjoy during the hot summer months!

Story

This recipe is very dear to my heart, for I have actually used this (and variations of this) as part of a complete program of care to help clients heal from debilitating hyperacidity and reflux. According to Ayurveda, digestive imbalances like these happen to be one of the root causes of fatigue and poor metabolism.

'wildly' fabulous seafood salad

By: Ashley Anderson and Mark Guarini

Ingredients

6 oz (170 g) wild trout or orange-roughy fish, bones removed, skin on

1 lemon wedge (about ⅛ lemon)

3 sprigs of fresh dill, chopped

1 cup sprouts

1½ cups organic baby spinach or mixed greens

1 medium red or green pear, sliced thinly

¼ cup finely chopped organic celery

2 tbsp Mamma's Italian Pesto (recipe on page 61) or Avocado Pesto (recipe on page 62)

8 Kalamata olives, pits removed

OPTIONAL INGREDIENTS

½ cup wild baby shrimp, cooked (garnish)

1–2 tsp finely chopped fresh chives, to garnish

1 tsp capers

1 lemon wedge (about ⅛ lemon), to garnish

Directions

1. Preheat oven to 350°F.
2. Place trout or orange-roughy on a large piece of parchment paper, big enough to completely wrap the fish. Squeeze fresh lemon juice from the lemon wedge over fish. Top with dill sprigs. Wrap fish and seal with string or twine.
3. Bake for 15–20 minutes. Remove from oven and cool.
4. On a large plate, layer spinach or mixed greens, pear slices, and sprouts.
5. Flake fish. In a separate bowl mix fish, pesto, and celery. Place mixture on top of salad.
6. Top with Kalamata olives and serve as is or add any of the optional ingredients.

Serves 1

Nutritional Benefits

Sprouts are a great way to add enzyme-rich, mineral-rich, whole foods to your diet. They make every meal digest easier! They also carry virtually no taste, making it super fun and easy to add to any dish. Wild trout and orange-roughy are an excellent source of lean protein, providing the amino acid building blocks for neurotransmitters, digestive enzymes, and a whole slew of other functions in the body. This highly alkalizing salad is high in electrolytes, thanks to the celery and lemon juice garnish. Dill is a flavorful herb that provides protection against free radical damage and is a great source of calcium. Shrimp and fish are great sources of anti-inflammatory omega-3 fatty acids, and have a very low glycemic index, helping to keep your blood sugar levels in tip-top shape!

Story

Mark just loves seafood, especially fish! I think that's why his skin always looks so great and glowing. He says it's because he's in love but I think it's because he drinks lots of water, exercises regularly, and eats lots of oily fish! We love to infuse sprouts whenever and wherever we can. Since I bought myself an automatic green sprout farm that automatically waters sprouts, I've been hooked on adding sprouts to many of my dishes. We find that when you squeeze fresh lemon on top to make the finishing touches, the dish (and your digestion) come alive! Like a fish, you'll be 'caught' at first bite!

apple, arugula, and chicken salad

By: Dr. Natasha Turner

From The Carb Sensitivity Program

Ingredients

- 2 tbsp extra-virgin olive oil, divided into two 1 tbsp portions
- 1 large shallot, sliced
- 4 boneless skinless chicken breasts (approximately 4–5 oz (113–142 g) each), cubed
- Sea salt and pepper to taste
- 4–6 cups arugula leaves
- 1 green apple, thinly sliced (unpeeled)
- 2 tbsp chopped walnuts, toasted
- 1 tbsp goat cheese, crumbled
- Fresh lemon juice to taste
- 1½ cups cooked quinoa or other grain

Directions

1. In a non-stick skillet, heat 1 tbsp olive oil over medium heat. Sauté shallot for 3 to 5 minutes; remove from pan.
2. Add 1 tbsp olive oil and cook chicken, stirring occasionally, until just cooked through, approximately 5 minutes. Season with salt and pepper.
3. Remove the chicken from the pan and set aside.
4. In a large serving bowl, toss together the shallots, chicken, arugula, apple, walnuts, and goat cheese.
5. Drizzle with lemon juice.
6. Serve with quinoa.

Serves 4

Nutritional Benefits

Chicken breast is a good source of lean protein. Arugula is a peppery dark green leafy vegetable that not only adds a beautiful flavor to this dish, but is highly alkalizing to the body, keeping you healthy and vital. Be sure not to skimp on drizzling the lemon juice, as it's also very alkalinizing. Walnuts are a great source of healthy fats that are especially great for your brain and memory. A green apple is the perfect way to complete all the flavors experienced in this delicious meal. It is a great source of pectin and disease-fighting antioxidants.

Story

I actually had a similar version of this recipe at a restaurant in Vancouver while on the media tour for *The Supercharged Hormone Diet*. When I came home I tried to replicate it, and even add my own twist to the ingredients. Best of all, simply switching the green apple to a red apple or an orange or pear will create a different take on the recipe.

leafy waldorf salad

By: Jesse Schelew

Ingredients

SALAD

One 5 oz (142 g) box of mixed greens

2 Macintosh apples, chopped

4 celery shoots, chopped

2 cups of grapes, halved

1 cup of pecans, toasted in a frying pan

DRESSING

¼ cup grapeseed oil

1 tbsp plain yogurt

½ tbsp honey

1 tbsp lemon juice

Salt and pepper to taste

Directions

1. Whisk or blend dressing in a small bowl and set aside.
2. Place mixed greens in a large bowl and top with remaining salad ingredients, with the toasted pecans on top.
3. Drizzle with the dressing.
4. Toss salad before serving individual plates.

Makes 3 large salads or 6 side salads

Nutritional Benefits

This salad is full of whole foods that are sure to satisfy your hunger. It has a great combination of fresh fruits and vegetables that are easily digested and energy producing. Apples are such a common food but their benefits cannot be overlooked. They are high in fiber and the apple pectin in them has the ability to help detoxify the body. The pecans add a great texture to any salad and have good heart healthy fats.

Story

Growing up the Waldorf salad was one of my all-time favorites! However, as I started learning more about food and I began to study holistic nutrition, I realized that the typical recipes for this salad were not always healthy. I wanted to create a healthy version I could feel good about eating that was sugar-free and free of commercial mayonnaise. The best part is that I actually like this version better!

watermelon salad

By: Shannon Kadlovski

Ingredients

1 small seedless watermelon

¼ cup goat feta or soft goat cheese, crumbled

½ red onion, chopped

Handful of baby spinach, chopped

2–3 tbsp pine nuts

2–3 tbsp olive oil

Juice of ½ a fresh lemon

Sea salt and pepper to taste

Directions

1. Preheat oven to 350°F.
2. Remove rind and cut watermelon into small triangles or cubes.
3. Place watermelon onto a plate or into a bowl and top with red onion and spinach.
4. Line baking sheet with parchment paper and toast pine nuts in the oven for 6–8 minutes until light brown.
5. Add pine nuts to the salad and top with goat cheese of choice.
6. Combine olive oil, lemon juice, salt, and pepper in a small bowl and pour over salad. Toss and serve.

Serves 4–6

Nutritional Benefits

This is a refreshing and nutritious salad that is full of flavor. Watermelon is a hydrating source of immune boosting vitamins A and C. Raw spinach contains minerals including iron, copper, zinc, and selenium, and is a wonderful plant based source of calcium. The sulfur compounds in red onion not only add a punch of flavor, they help to reduce cholesterol and detoxify the liver.

Story

This salad makes my mouth water. The combination of juicy watermelon, goat cheese, and the crunchy texture from the pine nuts, makes this one of my favorite salad recipes. It is also so colorful and appetizing to look at, making it a huge hit at dinner parties. There is almost no preparation involved, which I also like. It's refreshing and sweet, and almost feels like I'm eating dessert instead of a salad.

kale slaw salad

By: Marni Wasserman

Ingredients

SALAD

1 bunch of kale (any variety), chopped into bite-size pieces with ribs removed

1 head small red cabbage

2 carrots

1 beet

1 fennel

2 tbsp hemp seeds

DRESSING

½ cup olive oil or hemp oil

¼ cup apple cider vinegar

Juice of 1 lemon

2–4 tbsp raw unpasteurized honey

1 tsp sea salt

Directions

1. Shred the cabbage, carrots, beets, and fennel in a food processor using the shredding blade. Alternatively, use a mandolin or hand slice into thin strips.
2. In a mixing bowl, toss in the shredded vegetables and the kale.
3. In a separate bowl mix together the dressing.
4. Combine dressing with raw vegetables and toss together until the cabbage and kale are well coated.
5. Allow salad to marinate in the fridge for a few minutes—or up to an hour, mixing in the hemp seeds just before serving.

Serves 15

Note

Full of color, texture and flavor—this is a highly nutritious salad, especially when it is topped with mung bean sprouts! PS... the longer it marinates the better it tastes!

Nutritional Benefits

The variety of vegetables in this salad results in a power-house combination of nutrients. It's important to include alkalinizing foods in our diet. The Standard American Diet tends to be very acidic and therefore leads to many unwanted health conditions. The great thing about this salad is that every ingredient is alkalinizing for the body, so it is great for boosting your alkalinity and promoting health. Also, the cabbage and kale are cruciferous vegetables and therefore help to prevent cancer, heart disease, and oxidative stress.

Story

People always ask what the best way is to enjoy cruciferous vegetables while still having them raw. I have always been a fan of a vinegar-based coleslaw, so I decided to take my favorite (colorful) cruciferous veggies, chop them up small and create my own take on coleslaw that can be eaten any time of the year!

avocado chicken caesar salad

By: Briana Santoro

Ingredients

SALAD

1 head of romaine lettuce

Topping possibilities: hemp seeds, mushrooms, living cress, green onion, homemade croutons (see note to the right), shredded carrot, red pepper, sun-dried tomatoes, etc.

Grilled Lemon Chicken, chopped (see recipe on page 148 — just make the chicken from that recipe, you don't need the quinoa/cilantro)

DRESSING

1 avocado

Juice of ½ a lemon

1 ½ tbsp olive oil

½ clove garlic

Celtic sea salt and pepper to taste

Sprinkling of cayenne and paprika

1 tbsp water

Directions

1. Prepare lettuce in a bowl (wash, dry, and tear into small pieces).
2. Blend all the dressing ingredients in a blender until smooth. Pour over salad and toss.
3. Top with chicken and desired toppings, and toss one final time. Serve immediately.

Note

To make my homemade croutons I toast 100% Rye with Flaxseeds bread (Dimpflmeier brand) until **well** toasted. I then brush the toast with olive oil, rub with a fresh clove of garlic cut in half, and sprinkle with Celtic sea salt, rosemary, and oregano. Chop the toast into 1 inch squares and voila!

Serves 4–6

Nutritional Benefits

Romaine lettuce is very alkalinizing and is a great source of vitamins A, K, and C. It's high in water content, low in calories, and packed full of nutrients. It's always a good idea to get a large amount of greens in our diet! Also, adding the avocado to the dressing provides a delicious dairy-free creamy texture and a boost of healthy fats.

Story

Years ago one of the guys I worked with ate a lot of Caesar salad. I think he thought that he was eating healthy because he was eating a salad. Sure, the veggies are great but the dressings usually used are horrendous! Since I'm a big fan of being able to "have your cake and eat it too", I decided to create a delicious healthy Caesar salad recipe—one that fuels the body with nutrition but tastes so good you feel like you must be breaking some health rule.

SOUPS

VEGETABLE BROTH	98
CHICKEN BROTH	99
ROASTED VEGETABLE SOUP	100
MEXICAN FIESTA SOUP	101
CHICKEN NOODLE SOUP	102
FINEST FRENCH ONION SOUP	103
SQUASH AND COCONUT SOUP	104
SPLIT PEA SOUP	105
SEAWEED SOUP WITH BLACK RICE	106
GUT HEALING TURNIP AND LEEK SOUP	107
SQUASH AND CARROT SOUP	108
SUMMER SLIMMING GAZPACHO	109
LOVELY LENTIL SOUP	110

vegetable broth

By: Briana Santoro

Ingredients

16 cups water

5 celery stalks, roughly chopped with the leaves removed

3 carrots, roughly chopped

3 onions, roughly chopped

4 bay leaves

1 tbsp apple cider vinegar

5 cloves of garlic, cut in quarters

Directions

1. Put all the ingredients in a big pot and bring to a boil.
2. Turn to a simmer and simmer for 1–1½ hours with the lid on. Strain and it's done!

Makes roughly 14–15 cups
(If you don't leave the lid on it will yield roughly 10–12 cups)

Nutritional Benefits

Store bought vegetable broths can contain a lot of unnecessary additives such as table salt, MSG, coloring agents, and other unhealthy preservatives and additives that increase shelf life and appeal. This broth on the other hand, provides just water and nutrition! The nutrients from the veggies seep out into the water and then you consume the broth. Fabulous!

Story

The first time I made my own vegetable broth I realized 2 things. The first was that I would never buy it again since it was so insanely easy to make myself. The second was that soups taste way better when the base is a broth instead of just water! Making a big batch and storing leftovers in the freezer for when you are making soup is one of my favorite kitchen tips!

chicken broth

By: Briana Santoro

Ingredients

Bones from 1 chicken carcass

Approximately 16 cups water

2 carrots, roughly chopped into large chunks

3 stalks celery, roughly chopped into large chunks

1 onion, roughly chopped into large chunks

4 bay leaves

1 tbsp apple cider vinegar

Directions

1. Put all the ingredients in a big pot. Make sure there is enough water to cover the chicken carcass.
2. Turn the stove on high and bring to a boil, then turn it down to a simmer and simmer for 3–5 hours. I usually let it go for 5 hours as it makes it more flavorful.
3. When it's done, strain it through a fine sieve or cheesecloth. Discard the bones and veggies.
4. Store in the fridge for 3–4 days or freeze it for future use.

Makes roughly 12 cups of broth

Note

This chicken stock is great as the base for the Chicken Noodle Soup found on page 102.

Nutritional Benefits

This is not just full of flavor; it is full of nutrients and health benefits. Bone broth helps with bone, joint, tendon, and ligament health because it's loaded with glycosaminoglycans. It also improves the health of our digestive system, thanks to the gelatin, and helps make our skin, hair, and nails look wicked sexy! Furthermore, it provides loads of calcium, magnesium, and phosphorous. The apple cider vinegar actually helps draw the calcium out of the bones.

Story

I often cook up a full chicken at the beginning of the week and then my husband and I will use the leftover chicken in wraps and salads throughout the week. I started making my own broth out of the leftover bones and using it in some of my soup recipes. Boy, am I glad I did! I find homemade chicken broth tastes way better than the store bought varieties and it is really easy to make.

roasted vegetable soup

By: Dr. Natasha Turner

From The Supercharged Hormone Diet

Ingredients

6 beefsteak tomatoes, halved and cored

2 carrots, cut into ½ inch slices

1 small zucchini, cut into ½ inch slices

1 large onion, peeled and sliced

1 sweet potato, cut into ½ inch slices

2 leeks, white and light green parts only, thoroughly washed and cut into ½ inch pieces

1 tsp dried thyme

4–5 garlic cloves

2 tbsp extra-virgin olive oil

Sea salt and pepper to taste

4 cups organic low-sodium vegetable broth (such as Imagine Organic Low-Sodium Vegetable Broth or make your own using the recipe on page 98)

¼ cup crumbled pressed organic cottage cheese OR 2–3 tbsp plain Liberté Greek Yogurt OR two 1 inch cubes of crumbled Allégro 4% cheese

Directions

1. Preheat the oven to 425°F.

2. Place the tomatoes (cut side down), carrots, zucchini, onion, sweet potato, leeks, thyme, and garlic in a single layer on a large roasting pan. Drizzle with the olive oil and season with salt and pepper. Roast until tender, approximately 45 to 60 minutes.

3. Once the vegetables are cooled, peel the tomatoes, discarding the skins, and transfer the vegetables to a large pot on the stovetop. Add the vegetable broth (add more broth or water if needed). Bring to a boil, then reduce and simmer for 10 to 20 minutes.

4. Use a hand blender to purée the mixture until smooth.

5. Ladle into four bowls and serve each topped with cottage cheese, Greek yogurt, OR Allégro cheese, as a source of protein.

6. This soup can be kept in the fridge for up to 3 days.

Serves 4

Nutritional Benefits

Tomatoes are an excellent source of heart-healthy antioxidants, especially lycopene, beta-carotene, and quercetin. They are also a source of vitamin E, which is an important fat-soluble vitamin and antioxidant. The mineral manganese is found in zucchini and helps the body metabolize protein and carbohydrates. Leeks look like a bigger version of a green onion and provide a good source of folic acid, which is important during pregnancy.

Story

Anyone who knows me well knows that I absolutely love soups. The challenge that most store-bought soups have (even the homemade versions) is that they are high in taste but low in protein. An old patient of mine sent me this recipe and after a few modifications—including the addition of a protein source— a hormone-diet friendly version of roasted vegetable soup was born.

mexican fiesta soup

By: Briana Santoro

Ingredients

3 lbs (1.4 kg) plum tomatoes

1 tbsp olive oil

4 cups vegetable broth (recipe on page 98)

1 tsp Celtic sea salt

½ tsp pepper

1 tbsp oregano

1 tsp coriander

½ tbsp cumin

¼ tsp cayenne

3 leeks (use white and light green parts)

One 14 oz (398 ml) can of black beans (I use Eden brand)

2 cups frozen organic corn

⅓ cup quinoa, well rinsed

Juice of ½ a lime

Chopped cilantro as a garnish

Directions

1. Cut tomatoes into quarters and in batches blend tomatoes in a high-speed blender until there are no chunks.

Note

If you do not have a high-speed blender you can peel the tomatoes, and remove their seeds, or use canned, crushed tomatoes (however, the canned version doesn't taste the same as fresh).

2. Place the puréed tomatoes, olive oil, and vegetable broth in a large cold pot. Bring to a boil and add salt, pepper, oregano, coriander, cumin, and cayenne. Turn down to a simmer and leave covered for 10 minutes.
3. Thoroughly wash leaks to remove sand and thinly slice.
4. Add the leeks to the pot and simmer for another 10 minutes with the lid on.
5. Add the black beans, corn, and rinsed quinoa. Bring it back up to a boil and then turn it down to a simmer for 15 more minutes, covered.
6. Add lime juice, stir, and serve with chopped cilantro sprinkled on top.

Serves 6-8

Nutritional Benefits

This soup is filled with lots of herbs and spices that are wonderful for boosting our health. For instance, cumin and cayenne are great spices for boosting metabolism and increasing energy. Cilantro is a fabulous herb that is very beneficial for detoxing and pulling toxic heavy metals out of the body. Lime is alkalinizing to the body and helps to stimulate the release of bile from the gallbladder, thus optimizing digestion.

Story

When we were putting this cookbook together my team told me that they felt the soup section was lacking a Mexican flavored soup. I headed off to the kitchen to create the perfect soup to fit this request. The cool part is that this resulted in my new favorite soup recipe! This is definitely a soup that eats like a meal. I say that because it is hearty but also because when you are eating it you won't want to eat anything other than soup. It's that good!

chicken noodle soup

By: Briana Santoro

Ingredients

½ tbsp extra-virgin, cold-pressed olive oil

2 onions, diced

1 carrot, diced with peel on

1 sweet potato, diced with peel on

2 stocks celery, diced

1 tsp oregano

1 tsp thyme

1 tsp Celtic sea salt

1 tsp pepper

12 cups homemade chicken broth (see recipe on page 99)

½–1 cup brown rice pasta depending on how much pasta you want in the soup (macaroni or penne is nice)

4 stalks of kale, spine removed and chopped

1 ½ cups chopped cooked chicken (I use leftover chicken meat from cooking a whole chicken but you could also buy breast or thigh meat and cook that in the oven or a pan for this recipe)

Directions

1. Put olive oil in a pot. Add onion and sauté until translucent.
2. Add carrot, sweet potato, celery, oregano, thyme, sea salt, and pepper to the pot and stir.
3. Add chicken broth. Bring to a boil and then turn heat down to medium. Cook until vegetables start to become soft (about 20 minutes).
4. Add pasta and cook for 10 minutes.
5. Add the kale and chicken to the pot. Cook for another 10 minutes. Serve and enjoy!

Serves 8–10

Nutritional Benefits

The ingredients pack a powerful punch of nutrition and are extremely beneficial at helping to boost our immune system. This is why this is a great soup to consume when you are feeling under the weather.

Story

When I'm feeling under the weather I get this intense craving for chicken noodle soup. One time when I was in the grocery store I decided to read the ingredient list on some of the chicken noodle soup products on the shelf. Have you ever done this? It will shock the pants off you! I'm in the world of nutrition and even I couldn't pronounce most of the ingredients in some of these products. I went home that day and created this recipe. It's great because it actually helps me get better rather than filling my body full of a chicken noodle science project.

finest french onion soup

By: James Colquhoun and Laurentine ten Bosch

From The Food Matters Recipe Book www.FoodMatters.tv

Ingredients

5 red (Spanish) onions, peeled

4 tbsp organic cultured butter

1 ½ to 2 liters of homemade chicken or beef stock (or you could use vegetable stock if you prefer)

Unrefined sea salt and freshly cracked black pepper

1 tbsp naturally fermented fish sauce (or extra salt to flavor)

2 tsp raw apple cider vinegar

Fresh or dried thyme leaves

OPTIONAL

Raw gruyere aged cheese

Directions

1. In a food processor, slice the onions very thinly. Melt butter in a large pot on the lowest heat setting. Add onions and 1 flat tsp of salt, stir and cover.

2. Cook over this very low heat for 1 ½ hours, stirring occasionally. Add stock, increase heat slightly and cook until just beginning to simmer. Turn off the heat and add fish sauce and apple cider vinegar.

3. Season with salt and pepper to taste. Serve garnished with chopped fresh thyme and a grating of raw cheese on each bowl (optional).

Note

Gruyere is a firm yellow Swiss cheese. If you can't find this, use your favorite raw aged cheese. Parmesan works well too.

Serves 4

Nutritional Benefits

Onions are high in sulfur, which is essential for the repair and rebuilding of bones, cartilage, and connective tissue and also aids in the absorption of calcium. The homemade chicken/beef stock delivers a delicious rich cocktail of bone-building minerals (calcium, magnesium, manganese, zinc, selenium, and many more!) that are released from the bones used to make it.

Story

We love this slow-cooked, robustly flavored soup. It's simpler and 'cleaner' than the traditional version and just as delicious!

squash and coconut soup

By: Briana Santoro

Ingredients

1 butternut squash, peeled, cut in half, seeds removed, and then chopped into chunks

1 sweet potato, peeled and chopped into chunks

2 carrots, peeled and chopped into chunks

2 onions, peeled and chopped into chunks

2 tbsp coconut oil

¼ tsp Celtic sea salt

¼ tsp pepper

1 can of coconut milk

6-7 cups vegetable broth (see recipe on page 98) (add more if it's too thick)

4 tbsp finely grated fresh ginger (I use a Microplane for this but you could just use the smallest holes on a regular grater)

Directions

1. Preheat oven to 400°F.
2. Place the squash, sweet potato, carrots, and onion in a glass baking dish or on a baking sheet.
3. Coat the vegetables with coconut oil (to make this easier you may need to warm the coconut oil first until it becomes a liquid). Sprinkle with salt and pepper.
4. Bake for 40 minutes (stirring at the 20 minute mark) or until the fork pierces through the squash easily.
5. When the vegetables are cooked, remove them from the oven and place them into a big pot. Add coconut milk, vegetable broth, and ginger. Using a hand blender, blend until smooth and creamy. Alternatively, you can use a high-speed blender, blending everything together in small batches.
6. Heat and serve hot.

Serves 10

Nutritional Benefits

The butternut squash in this recipe provides high amounts of beta-carotene, which helps with vision health. It also gives us a boost of fiber, calcium, magnesium, and potassium (even more potassium than a banana!). The sweet potato adds sweetness, but is actually lower on the glycemic index than the white potato, meaning it won't spike your blood sugar. Plus, the coconut milk adds delicious dairy-free creaminess!

Story

There is something about the flavor of coconut that brings a big smile to my face. Perhaps this is because the smell and taste of it reminds me of being in a tropical place. I am a huge fan of the heat and not so fond of the cold weather, so being reminded of a tropical place makes me feel warm and happy inside. This recipe is so great because butternut squash tends to be a winter food. However, the delicious addition of coconut milk makes it into a creamy soup that transports me to a warm sunny white tropical beach with crystal blue waters, a hammock, a great book in one hand, and a piña colada in the other.

split pea soup

By: Shannon Kadlovski

Ingredients

- 1 onion, chopped
- 1 tbsp olive oil
- 3–4 cloves garlic, minced
- 7 ½ cups water
- 2 cups green split peas
- 1 cup lima beans
- 1 ½ tsp sea salt
- 3 carrots, chopped
- 3 stalks celery, chopped
- 2 fresh white turnips or 1 potato
- ½ cup chopped parsley
- ½ tsp dried basil
- ½ tsp dried thyme
- ½ tsp black pepper

Directions

1. Add onion, olive oil, and garlic to pot and simmer for 3 minutes.
2. Add water, peas, lima beans, and salt.
3. Cover, bring to a boil and then reduce to low/medium heat.
4. Add carrots, celery, turnips/potatoes, parsley, and spices and continue to simmer for 2 hours or until tender.
5. Using a hand blender or potato masher, purée the soup until thick.
6. Simmer for another 20–30 minutes and serve hot.

Serves 6–8

Nutritional Benefits

Both split peas and lima beans contain a ton of fiber, folate, and isoflavones that promote healthy heart function, lower triglyceride levels in the blood, and help lower cholesterol. They are also a fantastic source of meatless protein.

Story

I love soup. I especially love thick, creamy soups that eat like a meal. This split pea soup recipe is great because although it takes some time to simmer on the stove, it does not involve a lot of work. Once the vegetables are chopped and the ingredients are in the pot, you can go on with your day and come back to it for quick checks.

seaweed soup with black rice

By: Tamara Green

Ingredients

- ⅓ cup black rice
- ⅔ cup water
- 2 tsp coconut oil
- 1 onion, peeled and chopped into chunks
- 1 small sweet potato, chopped in cubes
- 1 bunch of radishes, sliced thinly
- 4 cups water
- 2 cups asparagus, chopped
- 1 zucchini, chopped in pieces
- 2 cups kale, chopped with the spines removed
- ¼ cup dried wakame seaweed
- 3 tbsp miso
- Fresh basil, chopped (to sprinkle on top)
- Sesame seeds (to sprinkle on top)
- Tamari (to drizzle on top)
- Sesame oil (to drizzle on top)

Directions

1. Combine the rice and ⅔ cup water in a small pot and bring to a boil. Reduce to a simmer and cook for 15–20 minutes, until water is absorbed.
2. Heat the coconut oil in a large pot on medium heat and add the onions. Sauté for a couple of minutes.
3. Add the sweet potato, radishes, and 4 cups water. Bring to a boil.
4. Reduce to a simmer and cover, cook for about 8 minutes.
5. Add the asparagus and zucchini. Cook for another 3–5 minutes.
6. Add the kale and wakame. Turn off the heat, keeping covered for a minute.
7. Ladle out a cup of the broth. Stir the miso in until mixed well. Pour back into the pot of soup. Add the cooked black rice and stir.
8. Scoop a serving of soup out into your bowl. Sprinkle lots of fresh basil and some sesame seeds on top. Drizzle with tamari and sesame oil. Serve and enjoy!

Serves 4

Nutritional Benefits

Seaweed soup it highly nutritious, tasty, and mineral dense. There are many different types of seaweeds, the kind being used in this dish is wakame, which is a brown algae. It is high in vitamin A, calcium, iron, sodium, and contains some vitamin C. The rice and veggies provide a boost of fiber, while the coconut oil and sesame oil provide healthy fats that give us energy and beautiful looking skin.

Story

It sounds cool and exotic, will heat you up just enough, and takes about 20 minutes to make. Serve this as an appetizer or snack. You can also add your favorite type of protein if you want to make it a meal.

gut healing turnip and leek soup

By: Alex Jamieson

Ingredients

2 tbsp extra-virgin olive oil

2 medium leeks, or 1 large leek, tender green and white parts only, cleaned and sliced thinly

¾ tsp sea salt

3 garlic cloves

1 bay leaf

1 tsp tarragon

1 tsp dill

6 cups water

1 lb (454 g) of white turnips, cut into ¾ inch chunks

1 lb (454 g) of small red potatoes, cut into 1 inch chunks

4 cups Swiss chard leaves, trimmed and chopped

Directions

1. In a large saucepan over medium heat, warm the oil. Add the leeks, season with salt, and sauté until soft, about 3 minutes.
2. Add the garlic, bay leaf, tarragon, and dill and sauté for 1 minute more.
3. Add water, turnip, and potato. Bring to a boil over high heat. Reduce heat to medium and simmer, covered, until the vegetables are tender, about 15–20 minutes.
4. Add the Swiss chard and simmer until wilted, about 2–3 minutes. Taste and season with salt and fresh black pepper if needed. Serve hot.

Serves 2–4

Nutritional Benefits

Leeks belong to the same vegetable family as onions and garlic, and are great for helping with cardiovascular health. The turnip in this soup is fantastic for digestion and it helps boost our immune system and fight free radicals. This is because it provides a good dose of vitamin C, which acts as an antioxidant in the body and helps to neutralize free radicals.

Story

Most of my clients, and most North Americans, need to heal their guts. Many things including an unhealthy diet and taking too many antibiotics over the years have destroyed our healthy GI tracts leading to gas, bloating, constipation, diarrhea, etc. This soup is one of my mainstay recipes for helping people to heal their guts.

Squash and Carrot Soup

By: Marni Wasserman

Ingredients

1 medium onion, chopped

1 tbsp olive oil

4 cups vegetable stock or filtered water

2 cups carrots, chopped

1–2 cups butternut or kabocha squash or sweet potatoes, peeled and diced

2 medium apples, cored and diced

½ tsp sea salt

½ tsp cinnamon

1 tsp nutmeg

2 tbsp fresh grated ginger root

***For added nutrition and a balanced meal, serve with some brown rice and steamed green vegetables such as Swiss chard, kale, or broccoli and top with pumpkin seeds or parsley for added texture and color!

Directions

1. In a large soup pot, sauté the onions in oil on medium heat until they become translucent.
2. Add the stock, carrots, squash or sweet potatoes, apples, salt, cinnamon, nutmeg, and ginger. Bring to a boil.
3. Turn down heat and simmer for 30 minutes. For a chunky soup take 2 ladles worth of vegetables and 1 ladle of stock and blend in a blender or food processor until smooth, then return to soup pot and stir together before serving. For a purée soup you can purée the entire pot.

Serves 4–6

Nutritional Benefits

The carrots provide a good dose of antioxidants, help with heart health, promote good vision, and support healthy colon cells. The butternut squash also helps with vision health and it contains a high amount of fiber, which helps support digestion.

Story

Squash and carrots are my go-to warming veggies. I love puréed soups in the fall and winter and I knew the infusion of these roots, with the sweet flavor of apple, would be the perfect balance. Spiced with cinnamon and ginger, this soup hits the spot!

summer slimming gazpacho

By: Alex Jamieson

Ingredients

2 lbs (907 g) ripe tomatoes, washed, cored, and roughly chopped (dice and reserve a few pieces as garnish)

1 red pepper, washed, seeded, and roughly chopped (dice and reserve a few pieces as garnish)

1 cucumber, washed and roughly chopped (dice and reserve a few pieces as garnish) (if it has thick skin, e.g. a Kirby, peel it)

3 cups low-sodium tomato juice

2 cups water

1 garlic clove, peeled

¼ cup red onion, roughly chopped

¼ cup white wine vinegar

¼ cup extra-virgin olive oil + a little extra for garnish

Pinch of salt

A few grinds of freshly ground black pepper

Directions

1. Place all the ingredients in a high-speed blender and blend until smooth.
2. Refrigerate for at least 1 hour to chill and allow the flavors to marry.
3. Serve in chilled bowls with a few diced veggies and an extra drizzle of olive oil as a garnish.

Serves 2

Nutritional Benefits

Tomatoes are high in lycopene, an antioxidant that promotes healthy bones, improves heart health, and can help reduce cholesterol. Red peppers are a powerhouse vegetable loaded with vitamin C and have been shown to help increase metabolism. Cucumber helps rehydrate the body, improves digestion, and can help fight inflammation.

Story

Did you know that when you go to an Italian restaurant on a hot summer night and order a chilled bowl of refreshing tomato Gazpacho you may be getting a hidden dose of gluten? Many traditional recipes use a piece of bread to thicken the blend, so if you're sensitive to gluten, be sure to ask next time you eat out.

Gazpacho means different things to different people—basically it's a cold veggie soup with some vinegar added to it. This soup really 'pops' the taste buds and adds bright, vibrant color to meals, filling up your senses and your tummy with a variety of flavors and fiber.

lovely lentil soup

By: Dr. Natasha Turner

From The Hormone Diet

Ingredients

2 tbsp extra-virgin olive oil

1 sweet potato, peeled and diced

1 large onion, chopped

4 cloves garlic, minced

1 inch piece fresh ginger root, peeled and minced

1 tbsp curry powder

1 tsp cinnamon

1 tsp sea salt

1 cup dry red lentils

4 cups vegetable stock

2 tbsp tomato paste

Directions

1. Heat the olive oil in a large saucepan over medium heat. Add the sweet potato, onion, garlic, and ginger and cook until vegetables are softened.
2. Stir in the curry powder, cinnamon, and sea salt and cook for a few more minutes.
3. Add the lentils, vegetable stock, and tomato paste and mix well. Bring to a gentle boil, reduce heat and then simmer covered for 30 minutes or until lentils are cooked. Remove from the heat and serve.

Serves 4

Nutritional Benefits

The rich supply of fiber from the red lentils in this recipe is a healthy way to improve digestion and also help you feel full for longer. In addition, sweet potatoes are high in beta-carotene and contribute to healthy eyesight and glowing skin.

Story

Of all my recipes I believe this one is the favorite amongst my patients. It's a great recipe on a cool winter day and the taste is divine. As a bonus, it includes great immune-boosting ingredients, such as ginger and curry, so it can help you get over a cold.

sides

SWEET POTATO FRIES	112
BALSAMIC RICE AND SUMMER VEGETABLES	113
TAHINI BRUSSELS SPROUTS	114
LEMON BAKED TOFU	115
CREAMY RICE AND KALE "RISOTTO"	116
MOCK MASHED POTATOES (RICH N' CREAMY)	117
RAW ONION RINGS	118
ASIAN COLESLAW	119
OVEN ROASTED TOMATO LENTILS	120
HIGH PROTEIN SUPER GREENS SIDE DISH	121

sweet potato fries

By: James Colquhoun and Laurentine ten Bosch

From The Food Matters Recipe Book www.FoodMatters.tv

Ingredients

2 medium sweet potatoes, peeled (approx 1.7 lb / 750 g)

3 or 4 tbsp coconut oil

Unrefined sea salt

Mild or sweet paprika

Directions

1. Preheat oven to 410°F. Cut sweet potato into ½ inch thick fries.
2. Line a baking tray with parchment paper. Toss chips on the tray with coconut oil to coat (melt first if necessary). Arrange chips so they are not over crowded on the tray. Sprinkle generously with sea salt and dust with paprika.
3. Bake for 10 minutes. Remove from oven, turn each chip over and return to oven. Bake for a further 10 to 15 minutes, until golden on the outside and soft in the middle.

Serves 3–4 as a side dish

Variations

Try making fries out of other root vegetables like parsnips, celeriac, and carrots.

Note

This is a high temperature to cook at, so if you have the time, bake them at 250°F instead. You will just have to allow much longer (maybe an hour or two) for the chips to become golden. Cooking at a lower temperature helps to prevent heat sensitive nutrients from becoming damaged or destroyed.

Nutritional Benefits

Baked in coconut oil and devoid of trans fats, this makes a nutritious and tastier alternative to the usual.

Story

We love to serve these delicious fries with tomato sauce or a quick guacamole of mashed avocado, lime, and salt. They are also fantastic when served with fish (like the Cod Piccata on page 153). It makes for the best ever fish and chips!

balsamic rice and summer vegetables

By: Connie Jeon

Ingredients

1 small shallot, chopped

2 tbsp chopped flat-leaf parsley

2 tbsp red wine vinegar

2 tsp fresh thyme leaves

Kosher salt and freshly ground pepper

⅓ cup extra-virgin olive oil

2 cups cooked basmati rice, cooled

2 cups assorted vegetables, cut into bite-size pieces (such as radishes, tomatoes, peas, summer squash, organic corn, shiitake mushrooms, carrot, etc.)

¾ cup torn mixed leafy greens, sprouts, and herbs

⅓ cup chopped red, yellow, or white onion or scallions

2 tbsp toasted pine nuts (optional)

Directions

1. Pulse shallot, parsley, red wine vinegar, and thyme in a blender until combined. Season with salt and pepper. With blender running, slowly drizzle in oil.
2. Process dressing until well blended.
3. Place remaining ingredients in a large bowl. Drizzle with 3 tbsp dressing and toss to coat.
4. Pass remaining dressing alongside for drizzling over.

Serves 4

Nutritional Benefits

This salad is a great way to get more greens in our diet. The olive oil will provide you with good monounsaturated heart healthy fats and will help you feel more satiated. Plus, the brown rice and veggies provide a boost of fiber.

Story

Rice is a common staple in Asian cooking but this side of rice with vegetables is complete with all the goodness of the bite-size veggies. Even my boys who are anti-vegetables can't get enough of this side dish. A trick for the kids is to make the veggies as small as possible so that they don't actually look like vegetables. So chop away and see which anti-veggie person in your life you can feed this dish to.

tahini Brussels sprouts

By: Briana Santoro

Ingredients

1 lb (454 g) Brussels sprouts

2 tbsp slivered almonds

Water for steaming Brussels sprouts

DRESSING

¼ cup tahini

¼ cup water

⅛ cup lemon juice

1 small clove of garlic, crushed

1 tbsp honey

2 pinches of Celtic sea salt

Directions

1. Put 2 inches of water in the bottom of a steamer and bring to a boil.
2. Peel off any yellowing leaves from the Brussels sprouts and cut into quarters.
3. Put the Brussels sprouts into the steamer and steam for 5 minutes. When done, briefly run them under cold water and strain any excess liquid.
4. Put the dressing ingredients into a jar and shake well.
5. Put the Brussels sprouts in a bowl and toss with dressing and slivered almonds.

Serves 4-6 as a side dish

Nutritional Benefits

Brussels sprouts are a part of the cruciferous family of vegetables. They help with detoxification, inflammation, cardiovascular health, digestive health, and antioxidant support. Tahini is a good source of vegetarian protein and healthy fat.

Story

Growing up I was never a fan of Brussels sprouts. To be honest, I'm not certain if I really didn't like them or if it was more the thought of them I didn't like. Nowadays, I like Brussels sprouts, but truth be told, served on their own they really aren't my favorite. I set out to create a sauce that was healthy and would make my Brussels sprouts taste unforgettably delicious. Sometimes a magical sauce is all you need! Now I crave these little green balls of nutrition. It's probably the sauce that I crave more than the Brussels sprouts but nevertheless, I now love them and eat them all the time!

lemon baked tofu

By: Connie Jeon

Ingredients

2 blocks firm or extra-firm organic tofu, well pressed to remove liquid (to do this, wrap tofu in paper towel and a dish towel, and put something heavy on top for at least 15 minutes to an hour)

2 tbsp gluten-free soy sauce or tamari

2 tbsp lemon juice

2 tbsp olive oil

2 tbsp Dijon mustard

1 tsp coconut sugar or maple syrup

1 tsp basil

1 tsp thyme

Salt and pepper to taste

Directions

1. Slice your pressed tofu into ½ inch thick strips.
2. Whisk together all ingredients, except the tofu.
3. Transfer to a small shallow pan or zip-lock bag and add tofu, coating well.
4. Allow tofu to marinate for at least 1 hour (the longer the better!), turning to coat well with marinade.
5. Heat oven to 375°F.
6. Transfer tofu and marinade to baking dish and bake for 20–25 minutes, turning halfway through and pouring extra marinade over the tofu as needed.

Serves 4–6

Nutritional Benefits

Tofu is high in vegetarian protein and low in saturated fat. It also contains isoflavones that may help ease symptoms of menopause. It also can be helpful at lowering cholesterol.

Story

My boys love tofu! It's one thing I can use in my Korean cooking that they love. This recipe is one of their favorites. They devour it! Although my boys are meat eaters, I'd like them to know the world of vegan living as I am exploring this world. Food is an experiment and I love the flare of this tofu. With so many flavors, I hardly miss the meat. Try it and see what you think!

creamy rice and kale "risotto"

By: Alicia Diaz

Ingredients

1 cup short grain brown rice

2 garlic cloves, finely chopped

3 cups water

1 cup cashews, soaked for at least 2 hours, then strained

½ tsp Celtic sea salt

1 tsp cumin

½ bunch of cilantro

Drizzle of olive oil

Juice of ½ a lime

½ tsp spirulina

1 bunch kale, chopped with spines removed

Directions

1. Place rice, garlic, and 2 cups of water in a pot and bring to a boil. Reduce heat and simmer covered for about 45 minutes.
2. In the meantime, blend together cashews, 1 cup of water, salt, cumin, cilantro, olive oil, lime, and spirulina to make a creamy sauce.
3. Chop the kale and add to the top of the rice pot during the last 10 minutes so it steams. Then remove from heat and mix together with the creamy green sauce.

Serves 6

Nutritional Benefits

The sauce can be made with or without the spirulina, but the reason I chose to include it is that many plant-based diets are super high in SO many nutrients but tend to be low in vitamin B12. This type of blue-green algae just happens to be a super potent source of B12 and numerous other vitamins!

Story

Oh yum, more creamy goodness! I love this recipe for its simplicity and balance of savory tastes and nutty texture. I stumbled upon this creation one day because I had no idea what to make and the only veggies I had left were kale (not uncommon since I LOVE kale) and the ingredients you see here. I love throwing things into my blender and seeing what happens. This creation came out even better than I expected!

mock mashed potatoes (rich n' creamy)

By: Ashley Anderson and Mark Guarini

Ingredients

1 medium whole cauliflower, roughly chopped (including leaves, stems, and florets)

5 roasted garlic cloves (with the peels on lightly coat garlic cloves with olive oil, wrap in foil, and bake at 350°F for 15 minutes—then peel)

¼ cup goat cheese (plain, or with herbs, if desired)

⅛ cup butter or ghee

3 tbsp 10% goat yogurt

½ tsp Celtic sea salt (to taste)

SPICE OPTION 1

Garnish with fresh chopped chives or parsley

Add dried oregano, thyme, sage, parsley, and/or marjoram to taste

SPICE OPTION 2 (INDIAN STYLE)

3 pinches of cayenne (or as desired)

1 tsp coriander (if possible grind it fresh by putting the seeds in a coffee grinder)

1 tsp cumin

½ tsp turmeric

½ tsp dry mustard powder

¼ tsp Asafoetida (it is also known as Hing and can be found at the health food store) (optional)

Directions

1. Use a steamer to steam cauliflower (steaming leaves more nutrients intact). If you don't have a steamer, cover the bottom of a large pot with 1 inch of water. Bring to a boil and toss in cauliflower. Cover and let cook for 8–12 minutes, until soft.

2. Drain water from cauliflower. Add cauliflower, roasted garlic, goat cheese, butter, yogurt, and sea salt. You can eat the dish just like this.

3. If you choose to use one of the spice options, add in the suggested ingredients and enjoy the added boost of flavor!

Serves 2-4

Story

Ash and I adore the creaminess of mashed potatoes. However, since following a healing gut holistic nutritional protocol with Ash, we've really become used to minimizing our intake of starch, potatoes being one of them. We love the texture of puréed cauliflower, but for the sake of this cookbook, decided that our recipe needed some revamping. Our mentor and inspiration, Briana Santoro, gave us some ideas of how we could boost the flavor and taste. Thank you, Briana! The roasted garlic adds an insatiable flavor that meets the goat cheese and goat yogurt, and SINGS! I think you'll be pleasantly surprised at how great cauliflower 'mashed potatoes' can be revved up, spiced up, and dressed up like your holiday favorite, minus all the starch. Family friends of Ashley inspired us to bring some Indian flavor variations to this mix. I think you will love the spice option 2!

Health benefits

Cauliflower might taste bland but this cruciferous vegetable shines bright with many antioxidants that help protect against inflammation and heart disease. It is also a good source of B vitamins and contains phytochemicals that help the liver neutralize toxins and expel them from the body, thereby assisting detoxification and reducing the risk of cancer. Turmeric contains a potent anti-inflammatory compound called curcumin, which aids in decreasing inflammation in conditions such as arthritis and Inflammatory Bowel Disease. Asafoetida (also known as Hing) is a cooking herb that provides relief from indigestion, flatulence, PMS, cough and cold, and has anti-parasitic properties.

raw onion rings

By: Melissa Ramos

Ingredients

- ¼ red onion, thinly sliced
- 2 tbsp coconut oil, melted
- 1 tbsp honey
- 5 tbsp ground flaxseed
- Pinch of sea salt

Directions

1. Mix melted coconut oil and honey together, toss in red onions and marinate for 20 minutes.
2. Take out onion slices and coat in ground flaxseed mixed with a pinch of sea salt. Place coated onions in fridge so mixture can harden slightly.

Serves 2

Tip

Soak the onions in water with ice cubes for 5 minutes as it helps to take out some of the 'bite' from the onion. You could also try using a Vidalia onion if you prefer that type of onion flavor.

Health Benefits

Onions provide us with many health benefits. According to Chinese Medicine onions are great for the lungs. They help increase lung capacity and the circulation of Qi (vital energy). This is definitely an amazing treat if you want to kick a cold or the flu goodbye.

Story

I can't help but love onion rings. It's the one savory "dirty food" that I crave. So I went out and sought an alternative I could be happy with. Granted this isn't deep-fried, but it sure will taste sinful anyway. The only word of caution is don't plan on getting up close and personal after eating this since raw onions can ward off a small army of men. If this is too strong for your tummy, opt for slightly cooked onions (in a frying pan or oven), which will make them less pungent.

asian coleslaw

By: Connie Jeon

Ingredients

SLAW

½ head Napa cabbage, finely cut

2 large carrots, grated

DRESSING

¼ cup creamy almond butter

1 tbsp apple cider vinegar

1 tsp Ume plum vinegar

1 tbsp toasted sesame oil

1 tbsp lime juice

¼ tsp finely grated fresh ginger

5 drops liquid stevia

2 tbsp sesame seeds

Directions

1. Place chopped cabbage and grated carrots in a large bowl.
2. In a separate bowl, combine the almond butter, vinegars, oil, lime juice, ginger, and stevia. Mix thoroughly.
3. Stir the sesame seeds into the dressing.
4. Add the dressing to the cabbage and carrots, and toss. Make sure that the vegetables are well coated. Serve.

Serves 4-6

Nutritional Benefits

Napa cabbage is low in calories and is loaded with antioxidants and fiber. Plus, it may help protect against breast, colon, and prostate cancers. Carrots are known for their ability to help with eyesight. The addition of almond butter adds a boost of healthy fats and protein.

Story

I love coleslaw but this is hands down my favorite! The unique mixture of the almond butter with the sourness of the two vinegars is what makes it so special. Try it and you'll see for yourself that it makes the perfect combination!

oven roasted tomato lentils

By: Tamara Green

Ingredients

2 to 3 cups grape tomatoes, mixed variety (local and organic are best), cut in half

4 cloves garlic, minced or chopped finely

1 tbsp grapeseed oil

1 tbsp balsamic vinegar

¼ tsp sea salt

½ cup French lentils (dry)

2 cups water

1 cup fresh basil, chopped

2 tbsp olive oil

Directions

1. Preheat the oven to 375°F.
2. Mix the tomatoes, garlic, grapeseed oil, balsamic vinegar, and sea salt together and spread out on a baking sheet.
3. Roast in the oven for 20–25 minutes, until the tomatoes are beautifully softened and roasted.
4. While the tomatoes are roasting, place the lentils in a pot with water. Bring to a boil and reduce to a simmer. Cover and cook for about 20 minutes, or until the lentils are soft.
5. Drain the lentils to remove any excess water.
6. Mix together the lentils with the roasted tomatoes and garlic. Mix in the fresh basil. Drizzle olive oil over top and serve.

Serves 3

Nutritional Benefits

Lentils are a great addition to anyone's diet and can be even more beneficial to vegetarians and vegans. They are full of B vitamins, protein, fiber, and help keep our blood sugar levels stable. Basil is rich in vitamin A and magnesium, which is helpful for relaxing muscles, blood vessels, and improving blood flow. Garlic is a powerful sulfur containing food that has many health benefits. It helps keep cholesterol levels down and blood pressure under control.

Story

Most people that I know love fresh tomatoes and although I am always eating vegetables, I am not the biggest fan of raw tomatoes. So, I started roasting tomatoes instead, which is one of the most delicious tastes ever, especially with some balsamic vinegar drizzled over top.

high protein super greens side dish

By: Ashley Anderson and Mark Guarini

Ingredients

2 cups baby bok choy, chopped (keep the bottom 'rose buds' for decoration if entertaining)

1 cup rapini or dandelion leaves, chopped

1 ½ cups cooked quinoa

14 oz (398 ml) can navy beans (we use Eden brand), rinsed and strained

⅓ cup Vegan Almond Basil Pesto (see recipe on page 60) or Mamma's Italian pesto (see recipe on page 61)

1 stalk organic celery, chopped and diced

1 tbsp extra-virgin cold-pressed olive oil

2 small pinches of dulse flakes

½ tsp Celtic sea salt

OPTIONAL

4 oz (113 g) organic tempeh, cooked and crumbled (to add more protein)

2 tbsp raw pine nuts

Directions

1. In a large bowl, combine organic navy beans with pesto of your choice.
2. Add all remaining ingredients and toss well so that pesto is evenly spread.
3. If entertaining, top with baby bok choy ends (aka 'rose buds'). Serve and enjoy.

Serves 2

Story

Mark adores rapini. If he could have one vegetable for the rest of his life both he and his dad, Marco, would probably put in their lifelong orders for rapini. Rapini, or broccoli rabe, is a dark green, mineral-rich leafy vegetable, often containing small broccoli-florets. When eaten raw, this vegetable can be very bitter. Cooking gives it a buttery flavor. Mark and I love looking for new ways to use rapini. We had some fun in the kitchen one Sunday afternoon, dancing to Frank Sinatra and Tony Bennett, and created this high protein vegetarian masterpiece. I love to garnish this dish with the cut bottoms from the baby bok choy because they remind me of 'rose buds'. Mark always calls me his little 'rose bud'.

Health Benefits

This recipe is filled with a complete essential amino acid profile. Yippee! This is important when creating and eating vegetarian meals to ensure the meal as a whole is a complete protein. A complete protein occurs when all essential amino acids are present. These amino acids are called essential because our body can't make them. We need to get them in the food we eat. Thanks to the beans and quinoa, this meal provides a complete protein. Organic dulse flakes and Celtic sea salt are a great way to sneak in some added minerals, especially iodine, which promotes the health of the thyroid. Dandelion leaves provide great support for the liver. Use dandelion leaves to support liver detoxification and liver health. Tempeh is optional and is a great source of non-dairy probiotics.

vegetarian mains

GLUTEN-FREE LENTIL AND SQUASH LASAGNA	124
EASY MAC AND CHEESE	126
ROASTED VEGGIE ALMOND TART	127
RAW PAD THAI	128
VEGGIE SUSHI	129
SPICY LENTIL BURGERS	130
MEXICAN (TACO) BOWL	131
BLACK BEAN YUM TUM STEW	132
AUTUMN HARVEST CURRY BOWL	133
BROWN RICE PASTA WITH PEAS AND RICOTTA	134
DAIRY-FREE ZUCCHINI ALFREDO	135
EGGPLANT HUMMUS MEDALLIONS	136
BEET QUINOA VEGGIE BURGER	137
BAKED "TUNA" CASSEROLE	138
MUNG BEANS AND QUINOA	139
CORN AND KIDNEY BEAN CHILI	140
CURRIED CHICKPEAS WITH KALE AND QUINOA	141

gluten-free lentil and squash lasagna

By: Briana Santoro

Ingredients

1 small squash (you will need 2½ cups of mashed squash)

1 cup water + ½ cup water

2 tbsp + 1 tsp olive oil

1 onion, diced

3 cloves garlic, crushed

8 oz (227 g) white mushrooms, sliced (approximately 16 small mushrooms)

1 green zucchini, diced

½ cup brown lentils (dry)

1 tsp Celtic sea salt

½ tsp pepper

½ tbsp basil

½ tbsp oregano

One 28 oz (796 ml) can of crushed tomatoes

5.3 oz (150 g) soft goat cheese

2 cups (200 g) goat feta, crumbled

One 10 oz (280g) box brown rice noodles—approximately 12 noodles (I use Tinkyada brand)

Directions to Prepare the Lasagna:

1. Preheat oven to 400°F.
2. **Preparing the squash layer:** Cut squash in half and remove seeds. Place face down in a baking dish with 1 cup water. Bake for 45 minutes to 1 hour, or until easily pierced with a fork. Peel off skin and discard. Cut squash into chunks and mash with potato masher. Measure out 2½ cups and set aside.
3. **Preparing the tomato sauce layer:** In a medium size pot on medium heat add 2 tbsp olive oil, onion, and garlic. Sauté until translucent. Add mushrooms and zucchini and cook for 5 minutes. Add lentils, sea salt, pepper, basil, and oregano. Stir and leave on heat for 5 minutes, stirring occasionally. Add can of tomatoes, stir, cover, and cook for about 45 minutes, or until lentils are cooked. Stir occasionally.
4. **Preparing the cheese layer:** In a bowl mix together soft goat cheese and ½ cup water until smooth. Set aside. Crumble the feta into a separate bowl and set aside.
5. Cook brown rice lasagna noodles according to instructions on the box.
6. It's time to assemble the lasagna.

   Layer 1 = ⅓ of the tomato sauce

   Layer 2 = 3 noodles

   Layer 3 = ½ of the squash

   Layer 4 = 3 noodles

   Layer 5 = ⅓ of the tomato sauce + all the smooth goat cheese + ½ the goat feta

   Layer 6 = 3 noodles

   Layer 7 = ½ the squash

   Layer 8 = 3 noodles

   Layer 9 = remaining tomato sauce + rest of the feta

   The lasagna is ready for cooking. You can store it for up to 2 days in the fridge. »

Directions to Cook Lasagna:

1. Preheat oven to 400°F.
2. Cover with tinfoil and bake on medium heat for approximately 45 minutes (or until hot in the centre). Remove the tinfoil and cook for another 10 minutes. Remove from oven and let rest for 10 minutes. Serve and enjoy!

Serves 8–10

Note

To make this dairy-free create your own nut cheese with sunflower seeds, macadamia nuts or cashews. Also, to make this grain-free make zucchini noodles using a mandoline instead of the rice noodles (this was a great trick taught to me by my good friend Estelle).

Nutritional Benefits

The lentils provide a good punch of protein. The goat cheese also provides protein and tends to be easier for people to digest than cow's dairy. The brown rice noodles make this dish high in fiber and are an easily digestible grain.

Story

Truth be told, lasagna is one of my favorite foods! The problem is that I try to avoid gluten and cow's dairy because they don't agree with my digestive system. I decided that I wasn't going to let those two ingredients slow me down. I set out to create lasagna that was made with brown rice noodles and goat's cheese. The result was amazing. Plus after eating it, my digestive system and I are still friends, which is always a good thing.

easy mac and cheese

By: Marni Wasserman

Ingredients

1 lb (454 g) brown rice elbow pasta *(aka macaroni noodles)*

1¼ cups water

1 cup plain rice milk or almond milk (may use other non-dairy milk)

1 softened <u>small</u> butternut squash with the skin and seeds removed, cut in cubes, and steamed or roasted until cooked (if squash is large just use half of it)

½ cup nutritional yeast

3 tbsp arrowroot powder

1 tbsp lemon juice

1 tsp salt (or more to taste)

½ tsp garlic powder

1 tsp onion powder

½ tsp dry mustard

½ tsp smoked paprika

½ tsp turmeric

2 tbsp tahini

1 tsp mellow white miso (or additional salt)

Directions

1. Put the pasta on to boil, according to package directions. While it's cooking, blend all remaining ingredients together in a high-speed blender.
2. When the pasta is al dente, drain it, reserving about ½ cup of the cooking water, and return pasta to the pot.
3. Add the sauce mixture and cook, stirring, until mixture boils and thickens. Add a little of the pasta water if more moistness is needed.
4. If the sauce is not as flavorful as you'd like, add a little more mustard and onion powder.

Serves 8–10

Story

Bringing back my favorite childhood meal helps me to conquer my recent cravings for mac n' cheese. There is nothing more delicious than biting into creamy "cheesy" noodles that are doused in orange sauce. It's even better when it is vegan, gluten-free, and organic! After trying many non-dairy and other versions of mac n' cheese, I finally came up with a recipe that works. It has been tested on friends, family members, and my young cousins (who are very well acquainted with the traditional mac n' cheese). Only happy smiles and second helpings have proved to me that I have hit the mark!

Nutritional Benefits

Many people have a hard time digesting dairy. This recipe is great because it provides a dairy-free option that is kinder to our digestive system. The cheesy orange color comes from the delicious squash, which is a rich source of antioxidants and provides anti-inflammatory benefits. This can be helpful for preventing cancer, heart disease, and diabetes.

roasted veggie almond tart

By: Tamara Green

Ingredients

FILLING

7 asparagus stalks, chopped

1 zucchini, chopped

1 small sweet potato, sliced in thin discs

½ red onion, chopped

2 tsp grapeseed oil

⅛ tsp sea salt

2 tsp dried or fresh rosemary

1 tsp dried or fresh thyme

½ butternut or kabocha squash

1 cup arugula, chopped

CRUST

1 cup almond flour

1 cup oat flour or flour of your choice

2 tbsp sesame seeds

½ tsp sea salt

4 tbsp olive oil

A few tsp of water

Directions

1. Preheat oven to 350°F.

2. Spread the asparagus, zucchini, sweet potato, and red onion out in a baking dish and toss with grapeseed oil, sea salt, rosemary, and thyme. Roast for 15-25 minutes, or until done.

3. While the veggies are cooking, peel, remove seeds, and cut the squash into chunks. Steam the squash in a small pot for about 10 minutes or until it is soft. Then mash and set aside.

4. Prepare the crust. Mix dry ingredients together. Slowly mix in the olive oil. Add water gradually to make into dough. Press into a circular baking dish. Bake the crust for 5 minutes.

5. Fill the crust with mashed squash and then pour the vegetables over top. Sprinkle on some chopped arugula and enjoy.

Serves 4

Note

You can reheat in the oven if desired.

Nutritional Benefits

Meals with a large combination of nutrients like this one make health more achievable in our busy lives. The gluten-free crust makes it easier to digest and the almond flour provides a good source of protein. The filling is full of colorful vegetables, which provide loads of phytonutrients.

Story

This roasted veggie tart is one of my favorite dishes. It's a classic warming dish with a flakey crust and is filled with deliciousness. Great for making in the fall or winter and in the summer and spring by switching up the seasonal vegetables in the tart.

raw pad thai

By: Julie Daniluk

Excerpted from Meals That Heal Inflammation: Embrace Healthy Living and Eliminate Pain, One Meal at a Time by Julie Daniluk. Copyright © 2011 Daniluk Consulting. Reprinted by permission of Random House Canada and Hay House, Inc.

Ingredients

- 1 medium zucchini
- 1 large carrot
- 1 green onion, chopped
- ½ cup shredded purple cabbage
- ½ cup cauliflower florets
- ½ cup mung bean sprouts or radish sprouts (spicy)

SAUCE

- 2 tbsp tahini
- 2 tbsp almond butter
- 1 tbsp lime or lemon juice
- 2 tbsp tamari (wheat-free)
- 1 tbsp raw honey
- ¼ tsp garlic, minced
- ½ tsp grated ginger root

Directions

1. Use a spiralizer (or mandoline, or vegetable peeler) to create noodles from the carrots and zucchini. Place them in a large mixing bowl and top with the other vegetables.
2. Whisk sauce ingredients in a bowl. The sauce will be thick, but will thin out after it's mixed with the vegetables.
3. Pour the sauce over the noodles and vegetables, and toss. This dish tastes even better the next day once the flavors have had a chance to blend.

Makes 4 servings

Nutritional Benefits

This raw dish is packed with detoxifying vegetables. Zucchini makes a wonderful substitute for noodles and boasts only 25 calories per cup. Cabbage and cauliflower both contain indole-3-carbinol (I3C), which helps to balance hormones by reducing excess estrogen in the body. Almonds are high in omega-9 and vitamin E, and make a great substitute for the typical peanut sauce.

veggie sushi

By: Briana Santoro

Ingredients

⅓ cup brown rice

⅔ cup water + more water for cooking veggies

1 small sweet potato, cut into long finger-like pieces

2 small beets or 1 medium beet, cut into long finger-like pieces

½ an avocado, pit and skin removed and cut into long skinny pieces

¼ cucumber, cut into long skinny pieces

1 carrot, made into long ribbons using a vegetable peeler

4 nori sheets

2 tbsp gluten-free tamari

1 bamboo roller

Directions

1. Put the ⅔ cup water in a small pot and bring to a boil. Add rice, stir, and bring back to a boil. Put the lid on, turn down to low, and simmer for 30 minutes or until rice is cooked.

2. Half fill a medium pot with water and bring to a boil. Put sweet potato and beets in the pot and cook until a fork can easily slide into them (about 10–15 minutes). Strain and set aside.

3. To make the rolls, lay out one of the nori sheets on top of the bamboo roller. Scoop on ¼ of the cooked brown rice and spread around. Put some of the sweet potato, beets, avocado, cucumber, and carrot on top creating a horizontal line of ingredients across the sheet. Put some water in a small bowl and keep it near your roll. Dip the tips of your fingers in the water and lightly run them across the top inch of the roll (do not make it soggy, you just want to lightly dampen the nori sheet). Start rolling the sheet from the bottom. Once you have it rolled up, cover it with the bamboo sheet and press on it firmly, sealing it into a cylinder shape. Don't press so hard that the ingredients squish out the ends.

4. Repeat this 3 more times, creating 4 rolls in total.

5. Cut the rolls into 6 pieces. Serve with gluten-free tamari for dipping.

Serves 2

Note

This also makes a great appetizer!

Story

I love going out for dinner and trying different types of food. Sushi restaurants are definitely one of my favorites. The problem is these restaurants often use white rice, which lacks fiber, and in some cases they add sugar to the rice. On top of that, I'm not a big fan of eating raw fish unless I really know where it came from and how it's been handled. It's so easy to get parasites from improperly cared for raw fish. Yuk! I wanted to create a recipe that would allow me to have the delicious experience of maki rolls, in a healthy way, and in the comfort of my own home. Success!

Nutritional Benefits

The star of this recipe is the nori (seaweed). It is filled with sea minerals and is really high in iodine, in addition to calcium, iron, and magnesium. You also get the benefit of fiber from the rice and the vegetables. The tamari is great because it is a fermented soy product and is beneficial for digestion.

spicy lentil burgers

By: Dr. Natasha Turner

From The Carb Sensitivity Program

Ingredients

3 cups cooked black/French lentils

4 large eggs

½ cup grated carrots

½ tsp salt

1 onion, finely chopped

1 tsp ground turmeric

5 tbsp ground flaxseed

1 tbsp extra-virgin olive oil

Directions

1. In a large bowl, combine lentils, eggs, carrots, and salt and mix for 1 minute. Stir in onion and turmeric. Add flaxseed, stir, and let sit for a couple of minutes so that the flaxseed absorbs some of the moisture.
2. In a heavy skillet, heat oil over medium-low heat.
3. Form 6 small patties, place in the skillet, cover, and cook for 7 to 10 minutes, until the bottoms begin to brown. Flip the patties and cook the second side for 7 minutes, or until golden.

Serves 2-3

Note

Serve with vegetables or a large mixed green salad topped with olive oil, balsamic vinegar, salt and pepper to taste.

Nutritional Benefits

Lentils, although mostly known for their rich fiber content, can also help to lower cholesterol, improve heart health, stabilize blood sugar, and increase energy. Lentils are also a great source of complex carbohydrates and vegetarian-based protein. The eggs add an additional source of protein and the turmeric is a fantastic anti-inflammatory spice.

Story

Much like protein pancakes, anything that can be made into a burger form is great for someone like me that is always on the run. I formulated this recipe in the Clear Medicine kitchen, in conjunction with our nutrition team. After a couple weeks of trial and error we ended up with the perfect lentil burger.

mexican (taco) bowl

By: Briana Santoro

Ingredients

2 cups water

½ cup brown basmati rice

½ tbsp + 1 tsp olive oil

1 onion, diced

One 14 oz (398 ml) can black beans, rinsed (I use Eden because they are BPA-free)

1–2 tbsp tamari

1 Haas avocado

1 tsp lime juice

2 pinches Celtic sea salt and pepper

2 cups chopped romaine lettuce

1 tsp red wine vinegar

½ a tomato, diced

4 tbsp salsa

2 tbsp goat yogurt (optional)

Organic blue corn chips (optional)

Hot sauce (optional)

Directions

1. Bring 1 cup of water to a boil in a small pot. Add rice and bring back to a boil. Turn down to a simmer for approximately 20 minutes or until rice is cooked. Fluff with a fork and set aside.

2. In a frying pan heat ½ tbsp of olive oil on medium heat. Add onions and sauté for 5 minutes. Add beans, 1 cup water, and tamari. Turn to high and bring to a boil. Then turn to medium, stir occasionally, and continue to cook on medium heat for 12 minutes or until liquid has mostly evaporated.

3. Scoop the avocado into a bowl and add lime juice, salt, and pepper and mash until well combined.

Note

You can also do this in a mini food processor.

4. In a bowl toss romaine with 1 tsp of olive oil and red wine vinegar.

5. To plate the dish, divide the romaine into two bowls. Top with rice, black bean mixture, tomato, salsa, avocado mixture, and goat yogurt (if using). Place a few corn chips around the side. If desired, sprinkle some hot sauce on top and enjoy!

Serves 2

Nutritional Benefits

This recipe is filled with dietary fiber from the rice, beans, and vegetables. Also, individually, rice and beans are not a complete protein. They are each missing important essential amino acids and therefore are not complete. However, what the beans are missing, the rice provides, and what the rice is missing, beans provide. Therefore, when eaten together they create a complete protein.

Story

When I was down in Florida with my husband's family I whipped this bowl up for dinner one night. When we got home my sister-in-law asked me for the recipe. I figure it's always a good sign that a recipe is a success when people start asking you for it! She and my brother-in-law love this bowl. They have even made it for me when I was over for dinner. If you own a sombrero, now would be a perfect time to pull it out!

black bean yum tum stew

By: Tamara Green

Ingredients

2 tsp grapeseed oil, ghee, or coconut oil

1 onion, chopped

3 cloves garlic, finely chopped

2 stalks of celery, chopped

1 carrot, chopped

1 sweet potato, chopped in cubes

½ tsp coriander

1 tsp cumin

1 tsp chili powder

3 tbsp tomato paste

4 cups vegetable broth

One 14 oz (398 ml) can of black beans (I use the brand Eden because they are BPA-free)

½ cup organic corn kernels

4 cups kale, chopped with spines removed

Large handful of cilantro, chopped

Directions

1. Heat a large pot with the oil on medium heat. Sauté the onions and garlic for a few minutes, until they begin to turn translucent.
2. Add the celery, carrot, sweet potato, coriander, cumin, and chili powder. Sauté for another few minutes, until you smell the aroma of the spices.
3. Add the tomato paste, vegetable broth, black beans, and corn kernels.
4. Simmer, covered, for 15–20 minutes.
5. Add the kale and turn off the heat.
6. Sprinkle fresh cilantro on top before serving.

Serves 3

Nutritional Benefits

Stews are a fun and easy way to get a range of nutrients and flavors. Black beans are full of fiber, complex carbohydrates, and protein. Fiber is good for bowel health and keeping us regular. In addition, fiber helps our digestive system excrete unwanted toxins from the body. Goodbye gunk!

Story

Stews and soups are delicious in the winter. This recipe is reminiscent of summer black bean salads that we love—fresh cilantro, local corn off the cob, black beans, and grilled veggies. We have turned it into a soul-warming winter version of heat and spice.

autumn harvest curry bowl

By: Alicia Diaz

Ingredients

1 tbsp grapeseed oil

¼ red onion, sliced

1 clove garlic, chopped

1 inch piece fresh peeled ginger, chopped

1 tsp cumin seeds

1 small butternut squash, peeled, seeds removed, and diced

1 sweet potato, cubed with skin on

1–2 cups water

1 tsp curry powder (or turmeric)

½ tsp ground cinnamon

½ tsp fennel seed powder

½ can coconut cream (or coconut milk)

Rock salt & pepper to taste

Directions

1. In a medium pot, sauté red onion, garlic, ginger, and cumin seeds in grapeseed oil on medium heat until the seeds start to pop or the garlic/onions brown.
2. Add diced butternut squash, sweet potato, and water. Simmer covered until soft.
3. Add remaining spices, coconut cream, salt, and pepper and continue cooking until hot. Serve and enjoy!

Serves 2–4 (depending on portion size)

Nutritional Benefits

Diced sweet potatoes and butternut squash are easy to prepare, grounding, and very nourishing to the body. The digestive spices promote nutrient absorption and the creamy coconut will leave your belly super satisfied with a warm smile. Sweet potatoes are also known in Ayurveda to boost the immune system and calm the nervous system. Squashes promote circulation and reduce blood stagnation (which is another cause of fatigue). So, consuming these delicious veggies can offer more energy to you through better blood flow!

Story

Any time I am craving a sweet, savory, creamy meal that is easy to make, this is one of my go-to's. It seems to me that many people think they need to slave over the stove to create a delicious curry dish, but this meal proves that theory wrong, big time!

brown rice pasta with peas and ricotta

By: Dr. Natasha Turner

From The Supercharged Hormone Diet

Ingredients

1 ½ cups brown rice penne, fusilli, or spaghetti (or another gluten-free pasta)

½ package frozen spinach, defrosted and drained

1 cup frozen baby peas

1 tbsp unsalted butter

1 tbsp olive oil

1 garlic clove, minced

2 ½ cups ricotta cheese

2–3 fresh basil leaves, chopped

Sea salt and pepper to taste

Directions

1. Bring a pot of water to a boil with generous amounts of sea salt added.
2. Add the pasta and cook until al dente. In the last few minutes of cooking add the spinach and frozen peas to the boiling pasta.
3. Reserving ½ cup of pasta water, drain the pasta, spinach, and peas. Return the pasta, spinach, and peas to the pot.
4. Toss with the butter, olive oil, garlic, ricotta cheese, and half the chopped basil. Add the pasta water to create a thin sauce that coats the pasta. Season with salt and pepper.
5. Serve in pasta bowls and garnish with the remaining fresh basil.

Serves 4

Nutritional Benefits

Brown rice is rich in fiber and stress-combating B vitamins. Spinach is rich in magnesium and iron, and is an excellent blood purifier. Also, cooked spinach is good because cooking it reduces the oxalic acid, making the nutrients more absorbable. Baby peas might be 'baby' but they are loaded with iron and fiber, and help keep our eyes healthy because of the rich supply of vitamin A and lutein. Ricotta cheese is low in fat and a great source of protein.

Story

This is a healthier take on the traditional Italian dish, minus the bacon. This gluten-free dish is full of texture and delicious flavor. Much like many of our other recipes, it was created in the Clear Medicine kitchen with the goal of developing a gluten-free option that can be used in the later stages of a detox.

dairy-free zucchini alfredo

By: James Colquhoun and Laurentine ten Bosch

From The Food Matters Recipe Book www.FoodMatters.tv

Ingredients

4 zucchinis

1 cup of raw macadamia nuts, soaked overnight in water with 1 tsp sea salt

Juice of 1 lemon

2 tsp tamari

1 clove of garlic, crushed

1 cup of cold-pressed, extra-virgin olive oil

¼ tsp cayenne pepper

A pinch of unrefined sea salt

½ cup filtered water

Directions

1. Peel zucchinis thinly with a vegetable peeler, so that they resemble fettuccine ribbons.
2. Blend the remaining ingredients and place over the zucchini ribbons as your sauce.

Serves 2

Note

Add nutritional yeast to your mixture for 'cheesiness' and additional B vitamins.

Nutritional Benefits

Zucchini is a whole food, water-packed, grain-free, gluten-free alternative to traditional fettuccine pasta. It is also high in heart healthy antioxidants like vitamins A and C, and a great source of the crucial electrolyte potassium. Soaking raw macadamia nuts helps our body absorb their nutrients better and digest them more easily. Macadamia nuts charge our bodies up with skin beautifying vitamin E and stress-busting, energy promoting B-complex vitamins (especially thiamin, riboflavin, niacin, and vitamin B6).

Story

This is the best pasta alternative ever. It's Laurentine's favorite! We also love to use the sauce from this recipe as a dip for raw vegetables or to roll up in nori sheets with shredded carrot and cucumber.

eggplant hummus medallions

By: Jesse Schelew

Ingredients

2 medium sized eggplants, cut into 1 inch thick medallions

6 tbsp olive oil

Salt and pepper

2 garlic cloves, minced

2 roasted red peppers, chopped

8 oz (227 g) spinach

1 cup bread crumbs (I recommend spelt or brown rice bread crumbs)

2 tbsp fresh chopped parsley

Hummus (see recipe to the right)

HUMMUS

1 ½ garlic cloves

One 19 oz (540 ml) can chickpeas, drained and rinsed

¼ cup lemon juice (½ lemon)

3 tbsp tahini

2 tbsp olive oil

½ tbsp cumin

1 tsp paprika

Salt and pepper to taste

3 tbsp water

Directions

1. Brush eggplant medallions with 4 tbsp olive oil and season with salt and pepper. In batches, place eggplant in a frying pan on medium heat and cook for 5 minutes on each side.

2. Meanwhile, heat 1 tbsp olive oil in a frying pan on medium heat. Add garlic and roasted red peppers, and cook until you can smell the garlic, roughly 2 minutes. Add spinach to the pan and sauté until the spinach has wilted, roughly another 2 minutes.

3. Mix breadcrumbs, chopped parsley, and 1 tbsp olive oil in a small bowl and set aside.

4. To make the hummus, place the garlic in a food processor and pulse until it is coarsely chopped. Add remaining ingredients, except for the water, and process until smooth. Water will make the hummus creamier; therefore, add it slowly until desired texture is reached (this may require more than 3 tbsp of water).

5. Place eggplant medallions on a baking sheet. Evenly spread the hummus on top of the medallions. Put the spinach mixture on top of the hummus and then lastly, top with the bread crumb mixture.

6. Place in the oven on broil until the bread crumbs are brown (about 5 minutes).

Serves 4–6

Nutritional Benefits

Eggplants are low in calories and high in the nutrients niacin and potassium. The hummus helps boost fiber and the garlic is good for lowering high blood pressure, atherosclerosis, parasites, and fighting the common cold and flu. If you are worried about garlic breath, you will be happy to know that the parsley actually helps to freshen breath, making the garlic odor less obvious.

Story

Like eggplant parmesan? Forget boring cheese and tomato sauce, these vegan eggplant medallions are a winning alternative. Low in fat and oozing with nutrition, eggplant has never been so dressed to impress!

beet quinoa veggie burger

By: Marni Wasserman

Ingredients

¼ cup sunflower seeds

1 cup cooked quinoa

1 clove garlic, chopped

2 tbsp chopped parsley

½ red onion, peeled and chopped

¼ cup grated carrot

¾ cup cooked white beans

2 tbsp grated beets

1 tbsp tamari

2 tbsp brown rice flour

1 tsp kelp granules

½ tsp mustard powder

½ tsp ground cumin

1 tsp sea salt

1 tsp tapioca powder

3 tbsp fresh parsley, loosely chopped

Directions

1. Pre-heat oven to 350°F. Line a tray with parchment paper (optional).
2. Place sunflower seeds in a food processor and grind until they make a fine flour. Add the quinoa, garlic, 2 tbsp chopped parsley, onion, and carrot. Pulse until combined.
3. Add the white beans and continue to blend until smooth.
4. Put this mixture in a mixing bowl and add the remaining ingredients. Stir until everything is mixed together.
5. Form the mixture into 8–10 patties.
6. Place on baking tray and place into the oven for 20 minutes (10 minutes on each side to get them crispy).
7. Alternatively, place the patties on a grill for 3–5 minutes.

Serves 8-10

Nutritional Benefits

Quinoa is actually a seed not a grain. It is great because it is a complete protein and is loaded with fiber. We also get fiber from the beans, brown rice flour, and beets. The beets themselves are extremely beneficial for our health and can help prevent birth defects because of the high amounts of folate. Beets can also help prevent heart disease and colon cancer, and can help with detoxification.

Story

I was hired once to come up with several versions of veggie burgers for a keen client who wanted a "protein" fix that was vegan. After playing with different bean, grain, and veggie combinations, this one stuck the best. Everyone who has tried it loves the texture and loves that it is versatile enough to serve on a wrap, salad, or on its own topped with avocado.

baked "tuna" casserole

By: Marni Wasserman

Ingredients

1 small onion, cut into thin slices

1 tbsp sesame oil

1 cup wakame, soaked in cold water for 5 minutes, removed and chopped

2 tbsp + 5 tbsp tamari

One 16 oz (454 g) package of brown rice noodles or quinoa spiral noodles (I like the Tinkyada brand)

½ cup tahini

¾ cup water

½ cup wheat-free/gluten-free/brown rice bread crumbs

Directions

1. Preheat oven to 375°F.
2. On medium heat on the stove sauté onion in sesame oil until transparent. Place wakame on top of onions. Add 2 tbsp of tamari, and cook for about 10 minutes until the liquid is absorbed.
3. In the meantime, cook noodles according to the directions on the package until done. Drain and set aside.
4. Mix together tahini, 5 tbsp tamari, and ¾ cup water until smooth. If the sauce should curdle, continue mixing.
5. Mix together onion and wakame mixture, noodles, and tahini sauce and pour into a 9" x 13" casserole dish. Cover with breadcrumbs.
6. Bake for approximately 20 minutes.

Serves 12

Nutritional Benefits

Using brown rice or quinoa noodles provides a gluten-free alternative that is easier to digest. The wakame is a great addition to this dish. It is an edible brown seaweed that is helpful for thyroid health because it contains iodine, is helpful for bone health because it contains easily absorbable calcium, and is helpful for heart health because it contains magnesium.

Story

I grew up loving tuna casserole. It was my go-to dinner for years. However, I let tuna go years ago and welcomed seaweed into my life. This made for a new beginning in terms of recipe development. The goal for me was to bring the sea into my meals without the fish. Combined with tahini and brown rice noodles, this casserole hits the spot.

mung beans and quinoa

By: Alicia Diaz

Ingredients

1 cup green mung beans (soaked overnight)

4 cups water + more for soaking beans

½ cup quinoa

2 inch piece of fresh ginger, finely chopped

4 garlic cloves, minced

1 tbsp curry powder

½ tsp each: turmeric, cumin, and coriander

⅛ tsp garam masala (or pinch of cayenne)

2 tsp Himalayan salt

Sesame or sunflower oil to taste

Directions

1. Soak mung beans overnight in water on the countertop.
2. Drain the beans, rinse, and place in a pot with 4 cups water, quinoa, ginger, garlic, and curry powder.
3. Cover, bring to a boil, reduce heat, and simmer until beans break open (around 30 minutes).
4. At the end, add turmeric, cumin, coriander, garam masala (or cayenne), and salt.
5. Serve with a drizzle of oil.

Note

This recipe works great as a stuffing for roasted squash.

Serves 2

Nutritional Benefits

In Ayurveda, this is one of the most perfect foods. It is a great source of protein, which is deeply nourishing and cleansing at the same time!

Story

My body sings a resounding "yes!" when I'm making a dish using mung beans. In Ayurveda, deep, total body detoxification and rejuvenation is called Panchakarma. Its cleansing protocols are unlike anything else I've seen in modern holistic medicine. There is a beautiful balance achieved when detoxing in a way that does not deplete the body or strip away its natural resilience. Mung beans happen to be one of the key food ingredients in Panchakarma. Now you can enjoy the delicious gentle detoxing and nourishing qualities of this legume at home as well.

corn and kidney bean chili

By: Alex Jamieson

Ingredients

6 ears fresh corn, husks and silk removed, or two 10 oz (283 g) bags of frozen organic corn

4 tbsp extra-virgin olive oil

2 medium red onions, medium dice

4 cloves garlic, minced

1 tbsp sea salt

2 tbsp chili powder

2 tsp cumin

1 tsp ground cayenne

3 cups cooked kidney, black, or pinto beans (or two 15 oz (425 g) cans, rinsed and drained)

One 28 oz (796 ml) can plain crushed tomatoes, with juice

Directions

1. Cut the kernels off the cobs and set aside, or remove the bags of corn from the freezer to begin thawing.
2. Set a large pot over medium heat and add the oil and onion.
3. Sauté for 2 minutes, add the corn, garlic, salt, chili powder, cumin, and cayenne. Stir well and cook for 5 minutes.
4. Add the beans and tomatoes to the corn and onion mixture. Stir well and cover.
5. Turn the heat to low and allow to simmer for 30 minutes.
6. Taste and add more salt, chili powder, or cayenne as desired.

Storage:

Refrigerate ½ of the chili in an airtight container to reheat and eat within 3 days. Freeze the remaining chili to reheat within 2–3 months. Remember to leave at least ½ an inch of air between the chili and the lid when freezing to allow for expansion.

Makes 10 cups

Nutritional Benefits

The beans are a good source of complex carbohydrates, fiber, and protein. Studies have shown that beans can also help reduce cholesterol levels due to the fiber content. The great combination of spices in this recipe helps to fight inflammation, improve heart health, and clear congestion from the body.

Story

Chili feeds the soul as well as the belly and this chili feeds everyone—vegans and omnivores alike. This tastes best when allowed to sit for a while, but eating it fresh out of the pot is great too!

curried chickpeas with kale and quinoa

By: Alicia Diaz

Ingredients

1 cup quinoa

One 15 oz (425 g) can organic chickpeas

2½ cups water

2 inch piece of fresh ginger, finely chopped

4 garlic cloves, crushed

1 tbsp curry powder

½ bunch of kale, spines removed and chopped

½ tsp each turmeric, cumin, and coriander

1 tsp Himalayan salt

1 tsp sesame or sunflower oil

Directions

1. Place quinoa, chickpeas, water, ginger, garlic, and curry powder in a large saucepan.
2. Cover, bring to a boil, reduce heat, and simmer for 15–20 minutes.
3. During the last 5 minutes, add chopped kale to the pot and replace cover.
4. Remove from heat, add remaining spices, salt, and oil.

Serves 2-4

Nutritional Benefits

Chickpeas (garbanzo beans) are a slightly cooling legume which make them balancing for conditions of hyperacidity and inflammation. They are also very high in minerals and have an affinity for nourishing the reproductive organs. You will find that chickpea flour (ground up dried chickpeas) is commonly used in Ayurvedic skin and beauty treatments.

Story

I almost always use bulk grains and legumes and soak them myself. Every so often though, it's just quicker and easier to use the organic canned version. This recipe is a delicious quick way for you to enjoy a gently spiced meal, without having to soak your legumes a day in advance. I like to vary this recipe by substituting cooked lentils or brown rice and mixing up what types of veggies I use. Use your imagination and get creative with it!

omnivore mains

AGAVE LIME CHICKEN	144
POMEGRANATE POACHED HALIBUT	145
CHICKEN CACCIATORÉ	146
SALMON, BROWN RICE, GINGER, WASABI BOWL	147
GRILLED LEMON CHICKEN	148
HEARTY TURKEY CHILI	149
ALL DAY GRASS FED BEEF OSSO BUCO	150
ROSEMARY SALMON STEAKS	151
FISH TACOS	152
COD PICCATA	153
CRISPY CHICKEN AND LETTUCE WRAPS	154
PARCHMENT PAPER SALMON	155
SHRIMP CAKES	156
CLAY POT CHICKEN	157
PESTO SALMON	158
MEDITERRANEAN CASSEROLE	159

agave lime chicken

By: Connie Jeon

Ingredients

1 whole organic chicken (2–3 lbs (0.9–1.4 kg))

1–3 tbsp extra-virgin olive oil

1 tbsp agave nectar (or pure maple syrup)

1 tbsp sea salt

Dash cumin

Dash chili powder

3 limes

2 onions

1 head of garlic

Directions

1. Preheat oven to 350°F.
2. Rinse chicken and pat dry. Place in a 9" x 13" Pyrex or glass baking dish, breast side down. Drizzle with olive oil and agave/maple syrup and sprinkle with salt, cumin, and chili powder.
3. Stuff one lime cut into quarters into the cavity of the bird.
4. Cut the other 2 limes into quarters and place in the pan. Cut the onions in half and place in the pan (I leave the skin on). Leaving the skin on the garlic, break the head apart and scatter the cloves around the pan.
5. Bake at 350°F for 45 minutes (or more) until the skin starts to brown.
6. Remove from oven and raise heat to 450°F.
7. Turn the chicken over so that breast side is now up. Bake for an additional 15 to 25 minutes or until thigh temperature (taken with an instant read thermometer) is 170°F–180°F.
8. Remove from oven. Carve the chicken and drizzle it with pan juices before serving. Serve with the onion and garlic from the dish (discard the limes).

Serves 6–8

Nutritional Benefits

Organic chicken provides a lean source of protein without all the chemicals (hormones, antibiotics, and the fertilizers and pesticides in the food they eat). Onions and garlic are great for your liver, helping liver detoxification run smoothly. Make sure you eat them with the chicken and don't just use them to flavor this dish. These foods can help prevent infection by fighting bacteria and viruses, and can help protect us from cardiovascular disease.

Story

This recipe is my personal favorite because not only is it easy to make, but there are so many possible variations when you start experimenting with different veggies and spices. Try the recipe a few times and allow your creative instincts to take over. You'll see that you can personalize the flavor for you and your family. I hope you enjoy it as much as I do!

pomegranate poached halibut

By: Julie Daniluk

Excerpted from Meals That Heal Inflammation: Embrace Healthy Living and Eliminate Pain, One Meal at a Time by Julie Daniluk. Copyright © 2011 Daniluk Consulting. Reprinted by permission of Random House Canada and Hay House, Inc.

Ingredients

2 red onions, finely sliced or diced

Eight 3 oz (85 g) fillets halibut (use 2 per person)

1 cup pomegranate juice

SAUCE

½ cup mayonnaise

¼ cup natural mustard

1 tsp nutritional yeast

Directions

1. Preheat the oven to 350°F.
2. Place the fish fillets on top of the onions in a large flat glass or stainless steel dish and pour the pomegranate juice over. Bake for 8 minutes for fresh fish, or 12 minutes for frozen.
3. Meanwhile, whisk together the sauce ingredients in a small bowl.
4. Remove baking dish from oven and turn broiler to low. Portion a tablespoon of sauce on each piece of fish and return to the oven.
5. Broil until sauce begins to thicken, about 5 minutes. Place fish on a serving platter and pour onions and cooking sauce over top. Serve hot.

Serves 4

Nutritional Benefits

Halibut is a delicious white fish that is exceptionally high in tryptophan (for neurotransmitter support), selenium (a powerful antioxidant), protein, and vitamin B3 (important for stress and cardiovascular health). Pomegranate juice is very concentrated with disease-fighting and cancer-fighting benefits. The nutritional yeast is a great source of vitamin B12, essential for our nervous system.

Story

When life finds me blindingly busy, I pull out this five-minute-prep-time recipe to save my sanity. Halibut is a popular white fish choice, but you can use any kind of white fish, fresh or frozen. Other excellent choices include tilapia, basa, cod, and haddock.

chicken cacciatoré

By: Melissa Ramos

Ingredients

2 chicken thighs (with skin)

½ cup brown rice flour

2 tbsp olive oil

3 garlic cloves, whole (skin removed)

2 green chili peppers, chopped

¼ cup Kalamata olives, sliced

¼ cup white wine

2 tomatoes, diced

1 tbsp honey

Directions

1. Dust chicken thighs with brown rice flour and set aside.
2. Add olive oil to a pan and turn heat to medium. Add garlic cloves and chili to the pan and sauté for 2–3 minutes.
3. Add in chicken thighs and brown on all sides. Add olives and white wine and reduce heat to medium.
4. Add tomatoes and honey and then turn heat down to medium low. Simmer for an additional 10 minutes. Serve on top of salad, sautéed kale, or rapini.

Serves 2

Nutritional Benefits

The benefit to this dish is that it's packed with protein and cooked in a base of fresh cooked tomatoes that are rich in lycopene, reducing the risk of cancer and macular degeneration. Put this on a bed of greens and you have an easily digested dinner that won't weigh you down.

Story

I have a sentimental feeling when I make this dish. It takes me back to Italy when I was heart-broken back in 2009 and travelled alone. Going to a cooking class in a 14th century village, I was taught this recipe from a "Nona" (grandmother) who at first scared me. Dying to win her approval, I aced this dish and I attacked her with a hug. In return, she actually smiled. Success!

salmon, brown rice, ginger, wasabi bowl

By: Briana Santoro

Ingredients

SALMON

½ lb (227 g) salmon fillet

1 tsp extra-virgin olive oil

½ tbsp tamari

1 ½ tsp fresh grated ginger

2 pinches Celtic sea salt and pepper

2 slices of lemon

Parchment paper

BOWL

¾ cup brown basmati rice + 1 ½ cups water for cooking

2 cups field greens

6 sundried tomatoes, finely chopped

3 tbsp pine nuts, lightly toasted on the stove if desired

¼ cucumber, diced

SAUCE

2 tbsp gluten-free tamari

½ tbsp fresh grated ginger

2 tbsp olive oil

1 tbsp tahini

1 tbsp apple cider vinegar

½ tsp wasabi

½ tbsp honey

1 tbsp water

Directions

1. Preheat oven to 350°F.
2. Place salmon on a piece of parchment paper that is approximately 16" x 16". Top with olive oil, tamari, ginger, salt, pepper, and lemon slices. Hold up the two ends of the parchment paper (the one closest to you and the one furthest from you). Holding the two sides together, gradually fold them down making 1 inch folds. Then, twist and roll each end, creating a sealed parcel.
3. Bake salmon on baking sheet for 20 minutes or until cooked.
4. Meanwhile, boil 1 ½ cups water. Add rice and stir. Cover, bring back to a boil, and then turn down to a simmer for 30 minutes or until cooked. Fluff with a fork and set aside.
5. To make the sauce, mix all ingredients in a small container with a lid and shake until well combined.
6. To assemble the bowl divide cooked rice into 2 bowls. Top with field greens, sundried tomatoes, pine nuts, cucumber, and salmon. Drizzle with dressing and enjoy!

Serves 2

Nutritional Benefits

Sexy bod alert! This dish may make you look sexier!! Salmon is a fantastic, healthy fish that is very high in omega-3 fatty acids, which help to reduce inflammation and make our skin look radiant and healthy. This dish also provides us with loads of fiber, disease-fighting nutrients, and is a healthy source of protein, fat, and carbohydrates.

Story

The first time I had wasabi in my salad dressing was like being slapped in the face with amazing delight! When I make this recipe, my friends and family go wild!! They absolutely love it. Just a hint that you may want to make double so that you have leftovers for the next day, as I'm pretty sure you are going to want more once you've given it a try.

grilled lemon chicken

By: Connie Jeon

Ingredients

2½ tbsp extra-virgin olive oil plus additional for drizzling

2 tbsp fresh lemon juice

½ tsp sea salt

½ tsp ground black pepper

6 large skinless boneless chicken breast halves, pounded to ⅓ inch thickness using a meat tenderizer or rolling pin

Coconut oil (melted so it's in liquid form) for brushing the grill

¾ cup plus ⅓ cup (loosely packed) chopped fresh cilantro

2 cups quinoa or couscous, cooked according to the instructions on the package

½ cup chopped toasted almonds (optional)

1 lemon, cut into 6 wedges

Directions

1. Place 2½ tbsp oil, lemon juice, salt, and pepper in a large resealable plastic bag.
2. Add chicken and seal bag, releasing any excess air; turn several times to coat.
3. Let stand at room temperature for 30 minutes. Alternatively, chill 1 to 3 hours and bring to room temperature before continuing.
4. Prepare barbecue (medium heat). Brush grill rack with coconut oil.
5. Transfer the chicken from the bag to the barbecue with some marinade still clinging and grill until just cooked through, about 4 minutes per side.
6. Transfer chicken to platter and let rest for 10 minutes.
7. Stir ¾ cup chopped cilantro into cooked quinoa or couscous.
8. To plate, place quinoa/couscous mixture on the bottom, then the chicken on top, drizzle with oil, and sprinkle with remaining ⅓ cup cilantro and ½ cup almonds (if desired). Garnish with lemon wedges and enjoy.

Serves 4-6

Nutritional Benefits

Grilling meat results in the creation of AGEs (advanced glycation end products), which can lead to inflammation based chronic illness such as heart disease, type 2 diabetes, and arthritis. Marinating the chicken in fresh lemon juice actually slows the formation of AGEs significantly.

Story

This is my go-to dish for entertaining. It is so simple to make yet incredibly delicious. I especially love the flavor of the lemon. The best part of making this dish is watching it disappear when my family and guests sit down at the table. It's always a huge hit! I know you'll enjoy it.

hearty turkey chili

By: Shannon Kadlovski

Ingredients

- 1 package lean ground turkey (organic if possible)
- 2–3 cups vegetables of your choice (zucchini, mushrooms, onions, peppers, broccoli, etc.)
- 1 large can/large jar of crushed or diced tomatoes
- 1 can of tomato paste
- 2 cloves fresh garlic, crushed
- ½ tsp sea salt (can add kelp powder as well)
- 1 tsp basil
- 1 tsp oregano
- 1 cup canned or cooked beans (I use a mixture of chickpeas and kidney beans)

Directions

1. On medium heat cook ground turkey in a pan on the stove (strain the excess juice once cooked).
2. Cook veggies in a wok with water, or steam them until they start to change color (do not overcook vegetables).
3. Place 1 can/jar of tomatoes and 1 can of tomato paste in a pot and heat on low.
4. Add garlic, salt, basil, and oregano to sauce.
5. Add beans to sauce and simmer for 5–10 minutes.
6. Add vegetables and ground turkey to sauce and stir.
7. Serve hot—can be eaten alone or on top of quinoa or whole grain pasta.

Serves 6–8

Note

Store leftovers in fridge for 2–3 days or freeze.

Nutritional Benefits

Turkey is a great source of the essential amino acid tryptophan, which is a precursor to serotonin. Serotonin is a neurotransmitter that helps us regulate appetite, sleep patterns, and mood. This chili is also loaded with lycopene, a carotenoid found in tomatoes that is a powerful cancer fighting antioxidant and is what gives tomatoes their red color.

Story

Turkey chili is my comfort food go-to. It's so warming and filling, and is the perfect hearty meal for a cold winter's day. What I like most about the chili is that your entire meal is served in one bowl, making clean up time that much quicker. It is one of those meals that seems so complex but is really easy to make. I like that I can make a big batch for dinner and have enough left over for a quick lunch the next day, with no extra preparation involved. Simply reheat on the stove for five minutes and it's ready to eat!

all day grass fed beef osso buco

By: James Colquhoun and Laurentine ten Bosch

From The Food Matters Recipe Book www.FoodMatters.tv

Ingredients

4 or 5 grass fed and finished beef osso buco cuts (shin cuts), approx 2.2 lb (1 kg)

1 tbsp butter

2 organic celery stalks, finely chopped

2 brown onions, peeled and finely chopped

2 carrots, finely chopped

3 garlic cloves, peeled and chopped

2 tsp unrefined sea salt

8 anchovies, bottled in olive oil or brine, drained. If you omit these, add more sea salt.

4 bay leaves

1 cinnamon stick, snapped in half

2 fresh thyme sprigs or 1 tsp dried thyme

¾ cup red or dry white wine (organic and sulfur-free/minimal sulfur)

4 ripe tomatoes or 1 cup of tomato purée out of a glass bottle

½ cup spring or filtered water

½ tsp cracked pepper

Flat leaf parsley, chopped

Directions

1. Preheat oven to 195°F. In a large heavy based cast iron pot, melt the butter on the stove top, over low heat. Add the celery, onion, carrot, garlic, and salt and cook gently until softened and translucent.

2. Add the anchovies, mashing them into the base of the pot with the back of your wooden spoon until the anchovies begin to 'melt'. Add the bay leaves, cinnamon stick, and thyme.

3. Pour in the wine. Increase the heat slightly and simmer gently for a couple of minutes so the alcohol cooks out and the liquid reduces a little.

4. Add the tomato and water, stir through and take off heat. Gently add the meat pieces and submerge them in the liquid and vegetables at the base of the pot.

5. Put the lid on and place in the oven to cook for 10 to 12 hours. For a quicker cooking time, set at 248°F. It will be ready in 6 to 8 hours. Best rule of thumb is to cook at 176°F minimum, 248°F maximum, and adjust cooking time accordingly.

6. If you're home at the time, halfway through you can turn the meat over for even cooking, but this is not essential. The osso buco is ready when it's tender and easily comes away from the bone.

7. Serve with the nutrient-rich sauce spooned over, a generous sprinkling of chopped parsley, a simple green salad and sauerkraut to aid digestion. And don't forget to eat the marrow! Any leftovers are even better the next day, just reheat gently on the stove.

Serves 4 or more

Nutritional Benefits

This is a particularly nutrient-dense meal. When cooked this way in a sauce at low temperature, not only is the meat more tender, the nutrients are retained, the proteins undamaged, and the fats protected from oxidation. Cooking meats on the bone adds additional minerals and gelatin to the dish. We recommend using beef rather than veal for ethical reasons, and that the meat is grass fed and finished, from cows raised naturally, grazing on open pastures in full sunlight.

Story

This is a great meal to put on in the morning and come home to for dinner. Just throw together a salad and dinner is done!

rosemary salmon steaks

By: Dr. Natasha Turner

From The Carb Sensitivity Program

Ingredients

2 tbsp extra-virgin olive oil

1 tbsp fresh lemon juice

½ tsp dried rosemary

4 salmon steaks (approximately 4–5 oz (113–142 g) each)

4–6 cups mixed greens

1 cucumber, chopped

Sea salt and pepper to taste

2 cups of cooked brown rice

Directions

1. Preheat oven to 350°F.
2. In a small baking dish, combine olive oil, lemon juice, and rosemary. Add salmon steaks and flip to coat. Marinate for 20 minutes.
3. Wrap each steak in aluminum foil and bake for approximately 20 to 25 minutes. Remove from oven and let cool slightly.
4. In a large bowl, toss mixed greens together with chopped cucumber. Add salt and pepper to taste.
5. Divide greens among plates and serve with salmon and ½ cup of brown rice per person.

Serves 4

Nutritional Benefits

The natural, rich pink color of the salmon steaks is home to heart and muscle strengthening benefits, as well as brain and nervous system benefits. This is mainly thanks to the high amounts of omega-3 fatty acids. Adding in the brown rice helps to boost fiber and the greens are alkalinizing.

Story

Having grown up in Halifax, many of the dishes I make include fresh fish. This is one of my favorite recipes that my mom used to make. It is an amazingly simple and delicious dish that is packed full of flavor and healthy fats, which is great for improving body composition.

fish tacos

By: Briana Santoro

Ingredients

FOR FISH

½ lb (227 g) cod

½ tbsp extra-virgin cold-pressed olive oil

¼ tbsp fresh grated ginger

¼ tsp coriander

¼ tsp cumin

⅛ tsp of each pepper and Celtic sea salt

½ tsp nutmeg

FOR CREAMY AVOCADO

1 avocado

1 tbsp goat yogurt (for dairy-free, use cashew cream on page 47 or eliminate altogether)

2 tbsp lime juice

2 pinches cayenne pepper, salt, and pepper

1 ½ tbsp chopped cilantro

½ tbsp tamari

OTHER TACO INGREDIENTS

4 organic corn tortillas

2 tbsp pesto

2 tbsp salsa

2 radishes, thinly sliced

1 cup thinly sliced Napa cabbage

2 tbsp goat feta (optional)

Favorite hot sauce (optional)

Directions

6. Preheat oven to 350°F.

7. Put fish in a small baking dish. Coat both sides with the olive oil and ginger. Mix coriander, cumin, pepper, salt, and nutmeg in a bowl. Sprinkle evenly on both sides of fish. Cover pan with tinfoil and bake for 15–20 minutes or until cooked.

8. In a mini food processor pulse creamy avocado ingredients until smooth (you can also just use a fork if you don't have a mini food processor).

9. Heat each corn tortilla in a dry frying pan on medium heat for about 15–20 seconds on each side. Place tortillas on a plate and top with pesto, salsa, fish, creamy avocado, Napa cabbage, radish, feta (if using), and hot sauce (if using). Serve and enjoy!

Makes 4 tacos (serves 2 with a side salad)

Story

I'm really into country music. For my bachelorette party, my wedding party took me to Nashville to celebrate. What a blast! One of the nights we were out for dinner I ordered the fish tacos. They were so lip-smacking delicious that I decided to create a fish taco recipe of my own when I got home so I could enjoy them as often as I wanted to—which happens to be quite often!

Nutritional Highlights

These tacos are a great source of good quality fats from the fish and the avocado. Corn is a very common genetically modified crop. Therefore, it is important to purchase organic corn tacos since foods that are genetically modified cannot call themselves organic.

cod piccata

By: Connie Jeon

Ingredients

1 ½ lbs (680 g) wild caught cod

½ cup blanched almond flour

½ tsp sea salt

½ tsp of each rosemary, thyme, and oregano

5 tbsp extra-virgin olive oil

5 tbsp grapeseed oil

1 cup organic chicken stock

¼ cup lemon juice

¼ cup brined capers

¼ cup fresh chopped parsley

Directions

1. Mix together flour, salt, rosemary, thyme, and oregano.
2. Cut the cod into 6 pieces. Rinse the cod pieces in water, then dredge thoroughly in flour mixture, until well coated.
3. Heat olive oil and 2 tbsp of grapeseed oil in a large skillet on medium heat. Add half of the cod pieces and brown well, about 3 minutes per side.
4. Transfer from skillet to a plate, and repeat with remaining cod.
5. Place plate of cod in warm oven while preparing the sauce.
6. Add chicken stock, lemon juice, and capers to the same skillet and use a metal spatula to loosen the browned bits and incorporate them into the sauce.
7. Reduce the sauce by half, then whisk in the remaining 3 tbsp of grapeseed oil.
8. Plate the cod, pour the sauce over it, and sprinkle with parsley. Serve!

Serves 4

Nutritional Benefits

Cod is a cold-water fish that is very high in lean protein, rich in healthy omega-3 fatty acids, and filled with energy-boosting vitamins, like vitamin B6 and vitamin B12. It can be a beneficial food for people with atherosclerosis, heart disease, and diabetes.

Story

I try to serve a variety of foods to my family. The favorite is anything chicken, but for the omega-3's I try to cook fish at least once a week. To me, cod is a difficult fish to make flavorful, but this recipe really delivers. I am now sold on cod. The best part is that my family is too!

Crispy Chicken and Lettuce Wraps

By: Dr. Natasha Turner

From The Carb Sensitivity Program

Ingredients

1 small green apple, diced (unpeeled)

¼ cup diced red bell pepper

¼ cup diced cucumber

1 tbsp finely chopped red onion

1 boneless skinless chicken breast (approximately 4–5 oz (113–142 g)), cooked and diced

¼ cup Liberté 0% Greek yogurt

2 tsp extra-virgin olive oil

Sea salt and pepper to taste

1 small head of lettuce (4–5 leaves)

Directions

1. In a bowl, combine all ingredients except for the lettuce, and chill for 1 hour.
2. Place the chicken mixture inside each lettuce leaf, roll into cylinders and serve.

Serves 1

Nutritional Benefits

Water is essential for our health. Without enough water our body can't function properly. We can get water from drinking it but we can also get it from the foods we eat, especially raw fruits and vegetables. Combining the chicken in this meal with the lettuce wrap, cucumber, peppers, and apple helps to boost the water content of our meal.

Story

I am a big fan of lettuce wraps! Not only can they be eaten as a meal or a snack, they enable you to skip the bread option without losing the taste. This recipe is particularly easy to make without a large number of ingredients. It's also one of those meals that can be created from leftovers and eaten for lunch.

parchment paper salmon

By: Melissa Ramos

Ingredients

1 salmon fillet

3 tbsp chopped fresh mixed herbs of choice

Juice from half a lemon

Salt and cracked pepper (to taste)

1 sheet of parchment paper
(1 foot long by 1 foot wide)

Directions

3. Preheat oven to 400°F.
4. Fold parchment paper in half and cut into half a heart. Open up to reveal a heart and place salmon that is marinated in all ingredients above the fold, then fold the other half of the heart over. Roll all sides under to create a little pouch, place in a baking pan and slide into the oven for 25 minutes on the middle rack.
5. Upon removing, be careful when opening the pouch since steam will be released and could burn. Take a fork and check to see if salmon flakes easily in the centre.
6. Serve over a bed of mixed greens of your choice.

Serves 1

Nutritional Benefits

If you decide to go with salmon, you'll be reaping the rewards of omega-3's and the anti-inflammatory properties it provides. It's rich in protein, which also makes it excellent for helping to stabilize blood sugar.

Story

I remember once dating someone who couldn't cook to save his soul. This was one of the very first recipes I ever taught him and it was foolproof. It's simple and easy to make for a date and the best part is, there's practically no mess. You can always sub in chicken instead of fish and cook it for the same amount of time. The good news is that if you do decide to opt for chicken and you have leftovers, reheating it will still produce a moist chicken versus something that is completely dried out.

shrimp cakes

By: Connie Jeon

Ingredients

1 lb (454 g) raw shrimp, peeled and deveined

1 red or yellow organic bell pepper, finely chopped

1 clove garlic, minced

2 tbsp scallions, thinly sliced

1 tbsp freshly squeezed lime juice

1 tbsp agave nectar or pure maple syrup

½ tsp sea salt

¼ tsp ground chipotle chili

1 egg

½ cup finely chopped cilantro

½ cup blanched almond flour

3 tbsp grapeseed oil or avocado oil for sautéing

Directions

1. Place shrimp in food processor and pulse until finely chopped.
2. In a large bowl combine chopped shrimp, bell pepper, garlic, scallions, lime juice, agave/maple syrup, salt, chipotle chili, egg, and cilantro.
3. Form mixture into twelve ½ inch thick patties, dip each in almond flour, coating thoroughly.
4. In a large skillet, over medium heat, warm 1 tbsp of oil.
5. Add 4 patties to the skillet and cook about 5 minutes per side, until browned and cooked through. Remove and place on paper towel lined plate.
6. Repeat two more times with remaining oil and cakes. Enjoy!

Makes 12 patties

Nutritional Benefits

Shrimp provides us with a good source of selenium (an important antioxidant) and omega-3 fatty acids (helpful for fighting inflammation and reducing the risk of diabetes and heart disease). Another benefit to shrimp is that they are very high in protein and the protein they have can increase the amount of cholecystokinin (CCK) in our intestinal tract. This is beneficial because CCK actually helps regulate our appetite and may play a role in helping us feel more full.

Story

These shrimp cakes are great because I can control what goes into them and ensure they are a healthy food for my family. I particularly love the nutritional value that this delectable dish can possess without missing a beat in the taste department. When I serve this up, I ask my family how it can get better than this? Their reply, "it can't mommy, you are the best!" I definitely love my shrimp cakes, and my boys. Need I say more?

Clay Pot Chicken

By: Briana Santoro

Ingredients

One 4 lb (1.8 kg) organic free-range chicken

1 small red onion or ½ large red onion, peeled and cut into ½ inch slices

1 sweet potato, cut into ½ inch slices

1 beet, cut into ½ inch slices

3 tbsp olive oil

¼ cup balsamic vinegar

3 tbsp honey

1 tbsp fresh grated ginger

2 pinches of Celtic sea salt and pepper

½ small orange, cut into two pieces

½ lemon, cut into two pieces

1 sprig of fresh rosemary

1 tsp Celtic sea salt

¼ tsp cinnamon

½ tbsp dry rosemary

Cooking Note

I cook this in a clay pot. If you don't have a clay pot you can use a roasting pan with a lid or baking dish with tinfoil on top.

Directions

1. Soak clay pot in water for 30 minutes fully submerged in the sink. Then dry it off.
2. Place onion slices at the bottom of the clay pot. Place the sweet potato and beet slices around the inside edge of the clay pot.
3. In a jar shake olive oil, balsamic vinegar, honey, ginger, and the 2 pinches of salt and pepper together until well combined.
4. Wash the chicken and pat dry. Stuff the cavity with the orange, lemon, and sprig of fresh rosemary.
5. Sit the chicken (breast side up) in the clay pot on top of the onion slices.
6. Pour the cressing all over the chicken and vegetables. Sprinkle the 1 tsp of salt, cinnamon, and dry rosemary on top of the chicken.
7. Put the lid on and place in a COLD oven. Turn the oven on to 400°F. Bake for 1 hour and 20 minutes or until juices run clear when chicken is pierced and meat thermometer inserted in the thigh reads 185°F. Remove the lid and cook for another 5 minutes to brown the top of the chicken. Let sit for 10 minutes before serving. Cut and serve with the vegetables in the clay pot and a salad.

Serves 6

Story

My husband and I started dating back in university. The first meal I ever cooked for him was a clay pot chicken. I had borrowed the clay pot from my mom, made a delicious chicken recipe, and as the story goes, once he tried my food he was hooked for life! For our wedding gift, my girlfriend Estelle (who I lived with at university) and her husband Justin gave us our own clay pot. Receiving this gift brought back some fun memories and inspired me to create this clay pot chicken recipe. If you are looking for love in your life, give this recipe a try. Who knows, maybe the clay pot chicken will work for you too!

Nutritional Benefits

The health benefits that we gain from eating chicken really depend on the quality of the chicken we eat. Unfortunately, many chickens these days are raised in factory farming operations, are artificially plumped up, are fed food that is not their natural diet, are medicated, and are not provided with room to run around (especially not outside). This results in meat that is fattier (contains higher amounts of saturated fat) and has far fewer nutrients like omega-3 fatty acids, and vitamins A and K2, which help prevent heart disease and osteoporosis.

pesto salmon

By: Jesse Schelew

Ingredients

3 garlic cloves

1 cup roughly chopped kale (with spines removed)

3 cups fresh basil, roughly chopped

¼ cup fresh oregano

3 tbsp sunflower seeds, toasted

¼–½ cup nutritional yeast

½ cup sunflower seed oil or extra-virgin olive oil

2 large fillets of salmon

Salt and pepper

Directions

1. Preheat oven to 400°F.
2. Place the garlic in a food processor and pulse until minced. Add the kale, basil, and oregano and pulse until finely chopped. Add the sunflower seeds, nutritional yeast, and oil and pulse until mixed.
3. Check salmon for bones, pat dry with a paper towel, and season both sides with salt and pepper.
4. Place each salmon fillet on a square of parchment paper and spread approximately 1 cm thick layer of pesto on top. Fold the parchment paper around the salmon creating a pouch. Seal the top by folding it over and twisting the ends to create a seal.
5. Cook for 20 minutes, or until the salmon is cooked through and flaky. Use the leftover pesto to flavor a side of broccoli, asparagus, or any vibrant cooked green.

Serves 4

Nutritional Benefits

This meal is well balanced. It has leafy greens, heart healthy fats, complete protein, and essential fatty acids. The Standard American Diet is very rich in omega-6's and very low in omega-3's. While both are important for health, having too much omega-6 can result in inflammation in the body. Salmon is a great source of omega-3 and helps to balance out the ratio between the fats. This helps reduce inflammation in the body, which is a trigger for most chronic diseases.

Story

The truth is that I am totally obsessed with pesto. I put it on everything! I love to eat it as a dipping sauce for veggies or put it on potatoes, chicken, crackers, and even toast! I figured why stop there. I love salmon so much that I decided to try a pesto salmon recipe as well. The combination of the two was a match made in heaven!

mediterranean casserole

By: Ashley Anderson and Mark Guarini

Ingredients

1 tbsp extra-virgin coconut oil

10 large free-range organic eggs, whisked

¾ cup red onion, sliced

¼ cup shallots, diced

2 ½ cups organic spinach or kale, spines removed and chopped

½ cup organic goat cheese (can easily omit if making dairy-free, or make cashew 'cheese' filling: soaked cashews, rinsed, drained, and blended with a pinch of salt)

¾ cup sweet potato, peeled and thinly sliced (approximately 1 medium potato), tossed in a bowl with 1 tbsp 100% pure maple syrup and ½ tsp ground cinnamon

½ cup thinly sliced zucchini, cut lengthwise into long thin strips using a vegetable peeler (sprinkle zucchini with 1 tsp Celtic sea salt to draw out water. Leave for 20 minutes. Pat and wipe dry with a clean paper towel; removing salt as available)

1 tsp dried oregano

1 tsp dried sage

2 pinches dulse flakes

1 head of roasted garlic, peeled and mashed (with the peels on, lightly coat garlic cloves with olive oil, wrap in foil, and bake at 350°F for 15 minutes, then peel and mash with a fork)

¼ cup fresh basil leaves, chopped

¼ cup arame, soaked for 15 minutes

Directions

1. Preheat oven to 350°F.
2. Grease a 14" x 10" casserole dish with coconut oil.
3. Place sliced onions on bottom of greased dish creating multiple layers until all onion slices (red onions and shallots) are used. Next, layer spinach (or kale), then goat cheese, and lastly sweet potato slices.
4. Place eggs, oregano, sage, dulse flakes, garlic, and basil leaves in a blender and pulse until basil leaves are puréed.
5. Pour over onion-spinach-goat cheese-sweet potato layers. Remove arame from soaking water, squeeze out excess water and sprinkle arame over top of casserole.
6. Bake for 35 minutes. Remove from oven. Cool for 10 minutes. Serve and enjoy!

Serves 6

Story

This casserole is easy and quick to make. We love to entertain with this dish because everyone always comments on how beautiful each piece looks from the side. We love to make a special trip 2 hours away to Prince Edward County, Ontario, to collect fresh organic eggs from the hens at Thyme Again Gardens, an organic farm run by two lovely women named Lori and Lorraine.

Nutritional Benefits

Organic eggs provide a good source of protein. Green spinach and kale are excellent sources of chlorophyll, great for supporting healthy hemoglobin and oxygen-rich blood. Red onions are one of the best food sources of quercetin, a potent bioflavonoid that scavenges free radicals. Arame and dulse are a rich source of iodine, a component of the thyroid hormones thyroxine (T4) and triiodothyronine (T3). Without sufficient iodine, these thyroid hormones cannot be synthesized, impacting metabolism in every cell of the body.

desserts

COCONUT BANANA BREAD	162
LIVING BROWNIES	163
VANILLA COCONUT MILK ICE CREAM	164
GINGERBREAD COOKIES	165
CARROT CUPCAKES	166
CHOCOLATE PUDDING POPS	167
CHERRY MACAROONS	168
SEXY CHOCOLATE TORTE	169
FIBER-RICH COOKIE DOUGH	170
DATE BLISS BALLS	171
WILD BLUEBERRY TART	172
HEMP FUDGE	173
CHIA SEED PUDDING WITH COCONUT AND VANILLA	174

coconut banana bread

By: James Colquhoun and Laurentine ten Bosch

From The Food Matters Recipe Book www.FoodMatters.tv

Ingredients

- 2 bananas; at least 1 heaped cup of chopped banana
- ¼ cup coconut oil, melted
- 4 organic free-range eggs
- 4 fresh dates, pitted and chopped
- 1 tbsp pure maple syrup or raw honey
- ¾ cup coconut flour
- ½ tsp aluminum-free baking powder
- ¼ tsp unrefined sea salt
- ½ tsp cinnamon powder

Directions

1. Preheat oven to 350°F. Mash bananas with the chopped dates.

Note

If the dates are quite dry and hard, soak them first in warm water.

2. Whisk the eggs until fluffy and then combine with the mash.
3. Stir through the oil and maple syrup/honey. Add the dry ingredients and combine well. Put mixture in a loaf tin, greased and lined with baking paper. The mixture will be quite thick; flatten and smooth with a spatula.
4. Bake for 35–40 minutes. Ready when a knife comes out clean and the edges are browned. Allow to cool completely on a wire rack before storing in an airtight container in the fridge. Or eat while still warm!

Makes 1 loaf

Nutritional Benefits

This recipe is a great way to use overripe bananas and provide your body with potassium, an important electrolyte for the nervous system. Coconut flour is a handy product to have on hand; it doesn't have the glycemic load of grain flours, and has no gluten or anti-nutrients. The only thing is that it doesn't yield the 'fluffiness' of regular glutenous flour, and might take some getting used to.

Story

This recipe is a big hit. Many people love banana bread but the common recipes contain grains, gluten, and refined sugar. We love this one so much because it doesn't contain these items and yet still tastes incredibly delicious!

living brownies

By: Briana Santoro

Ingredients

3 cups coconut flakes, ground (or 2 cups pre-ground coconut)

½ cup walnuts

6 Medjool dates, pits removed

¼ cup chia seeds

¼ cup cacao powder

2 tbsp coconut oil

¼ cup natural maple syrup/honey

¼ tsp cinnamon

¼ tsp Celtic sea salt

3 tbsp each of chopped macadamia nuts and sliced almonds (for garnish)

Directions

1. Grind the coconut flakes into a flour using a dry container from a Vitamix machine. Otherwise, use a food processor, or buy it already ground.

2. In a food processor, using the S-blade, process the walnuts and ground coconut together. Add the rest of the ingredients, except the macadamia nuts and sliced almonds. Process until ingredients are well combined. Put the mixture into a 9" x 9" pan and spread it out.

3. Scatter the chopped macadamia nuts and sliced almonds on top and push them in slightly.

4. Put the pan in the fridge for 30 minutes before cutting and serving.

Makes 12 small brownies

Note

If you store it in the fridge for longer, you may want to let it sit at room temperature for 5–10 minutes before serving.

Nutritional Benefits

Most brownie recipes contain fiber-less flour, loads of refined sugar, and unhealthy fats. These are so great because they use gluten-free coconut flakes and walnuts as the base, have health-promoting fats, contain chia seeds to boost fiber, and are sweetened with dates and maple syrup/honey.

Story

I love to see the shock on people's face when they first bite into this brownie. It's so yummy you will be shocked when you find out how healthy all the ingredients are. We often think of dessert as a bad thing, something that we shouldn't have. This recipe changes all that! I even made it as the birthday cake for my husband's birthday a couple of years ago and everyone loved it!

vanilla coconut milk ice cream

By: Connie Jeon

Ingredients

3 pastured egg yolks

1–3 tbsp honey
(depends on your sweet tooth)

¼ tsp sea salt

1 ½ cups coconut milk

1 tbsp vanilla

Directions

1. In a medium pot whisk egg yolks, honey, and salt together. Add coconut milk and whisk again until well combined.

2. Place pot on stove over medium heat, stirring constantly for 8 minutes. Be sure not to let the mixture boil. Remove pot from the heat and stir in vanilla.

3. Transfer contents of pot to a bowl and chill until cold. Process mixture in an ice cream maker according to manufacturer's instructions. When it's done, transfer ice cream to a container with a lid and freeze until firm (approximately 1–2 hours). Enjoy!

Serves 4

Nutritional Benefits

Coconut milk is a great alternative for those with dairy sensitivities or anyone who wants to switch up their regular dairy based foods. Coconut milk is derived from the meat of mature coconuts. It is rich in minerals (like iron and potassium) and important vitamins (like vitamin B3, which helps prevent heart disease). Nature's sweetener, honey, is a good natural alternative to the usual white or refined sugar.

Story

My two boys LOVE junk food! One of their favorite foods is ice cream. However, knowing what I know about ice cream I just can't justify buying it for them. There is way too much sugar, artificial flavors, additives, etc. I don't want them clogging up their arteries, so what's a mom to do but find ways to feed them the good without the guilt. This recipe does just that and is a hit with my boys!

gingerbread cookies

By: Tamara Green

Ingredients

- ½ cup dates, pits removed
- ¼ cup water
- ¼ cup + 2 tbsp coconut oil, melted
- 3 tbsp molasses
- 1 tbsp maple syrup
- 1 cup ground almonds (almond meal)
- 1 ½ cups whole spelt flour
- 2 ½ tsp ground dry ginger
- ½ tsp cinnamon
- ⅛ tsp nutmeg
- ⅛ tsp sea salt
- ½ tsp baking powder
- 1 beautiful very dark chocolate bar

Directions

1. In a food processor combine the dates, water, coconut oil, molasses, and maple syrup into a creamy mixture.
2. Mix the dry ingredients together in a bowl (not the chocolate bar). Mix the wet and dry ingredients together. It should form a sticky dough.
3. Place in refrigerator for at least 1 hour.
4. Once the dough has cooled, preheat oven to 375°F.
5. On a floured surface, roll the dough out as thin as possible. Using a cookie cutter, cut out cookies and place on an oiled baking sheet.
6. Bake for 12 minutes, or until crispy.
7. Cool cookies on a rack.
8. Melt chocolate bar in a double boiler. Dip the cookies into the chocolate and spread out on a plate. Cool and yum yum yum, enjoy!

Makes approximately 10 cookies

Nutritional Benefits

The almond flour makes a wonderful flour substitute and it increases the protein content. This boost of protein increases the time it takes to digest these cookies, which helps to balance our blood sugar and reduce the spikes and plummets in energy level. The coconut oil is great for baking because it remains stable at high temperature. It is also a wonderful source of lauric acid, a substance that has antimicrobial and antifungal properties. The use of molasses as a sweetener is great because it is a fantastic source of iron, especially good for women.

Story

This recipe was created on a snowy day in toronto. The snow was so beautiful it almost felt like I could be living in the country, far away from the city. Snowy days are always perfect for warm cookies and tea. This is a delicious, comforting gingerbread cookie recipe that is healthy and incredibly fun to make!

Carrot Cupcakes

By: Alex Jamieson

Ingredients

1 cup whole-wheat, whole-spelt, or barley flour

1 tsp ground cinnamon

¼ tsp ground nutmeg

1 tsp baking powder

½ tsp baking soda

¼ tsp salt

1 tsp pure vanilla extract

1 cup brown rice syrup, real maple syrup, or agave nectar

1 cup grated carrot

1 cup unsweetened applesauce

¼ cup plain, unsweetened rice, oat, almond, hemp, or soy milk

¼ cup grapeseed or coconut oil

EASY ICING

1 cup coconut butter (not coconut oil), warmed over low heat until it's easily spreadable

½ cup brown rice syrup

Directions

1. Preheat oven to 350°F. Line the muffin tin with 12 cupcake liners.
2. In a large mixing bowl, combine the flour, cinnamon, nutmeg, baking powder, baking soda, and salt. Stir well to combine.
3. In a medium mixing bowl, combine the vanilla extract, brown rice syrup, carrot, applesauce, milk, and oil. Whisk well to thoroughly combine.
4. Pour half of the flour mixture into the carrot mixture and stir well to combine. Scrape the remaining flour into the carrot mixture and stir well.
5. Spoon into the cupcake liners, leaving about ½ an inch of space at the top of each. Bake for 15 to 20 minutes or until a toothpick inserted into the middle comes out clean.
6. Remove the cupcakes from the pan and cool at room temperature for at least 30 minutes before icing.
7. To make the icing, combine the coconut butter and brown rice syrup, and stir well to combine. Spread over the cooled cupcakes.

Makes 12 cupcakes

Nutritional Benefits

Carrots are a very good source of beta-carotene, which is helpful for our cardiovascular and vision health. These yummy cupcakes are topped with coconut butter icing, which contains healthy medium-chain fatty acids that convert quickly to energy in the body. Remember, coconut butter is different from coconut oil. The coconut butter contains the meat of the coconut whereas the oil does not.

Story

Treats don't have to ruin your health. I make a dozen cupcakes at a time, freeze most of them, and take a few to parties when my son is invited to help celebrate a friend's birthday. The rest can be defrosted overnight in the fridge as needed.

Chocolate Pudding Pops

By: Connie Jeon

Ingredients

2 cups coconut milk, almond milk, or raw milk

2 tsp gelatin

Heaping 1 oz (28 g) food grade cacao butter (weight), or ¼ cup melted

½ cup cacao powder (keep in mind that cacao contains some caffeine)

2 ripe avocados, peel and pit removed

1 large ripe banana

¼ cup to ½ cup raw honey (your preference for sweetness)

1 tsp vanilla extract

¼ tsp sea salt

Nuts (almonds, walnuts, Brazil nuts, etc.)

Directions

1. Place coconut milk, almond milk, or raw milk on the stove until it is hot (but not boiling), then remove from heat and set aside.
2. In a medium mixing bowl add the gelatin and 2 tbsp of the warm milk to allow it to set up.
3. In a double boiler or small pot set over simmering water, melt the cacao butter completely.
4. Remove cacao butter from heat and stir in the remaining hot milk. Slowly add this mixture to gelatin, whisking thoroughly until the gelatin is completely dissolved.
5. Add this mixture and all other ingredients (except nuts) to a blender and purée until smooth.
6. Taste to make sure it has enough chocolate and is sweet enough for you. Add cacao powder and honey as needed.
7. Pour this mixture into a popsicle mold or Dixie cups with a popsicle stick and sprinkle base with nuts, if desired.
8. Freeze for at least 2 hours.

Makes approximately 6
(This depends on how big your popsicle molds are)

Nutritional Benefits

Avocados are rich in heart healthy fats and vitamin E. Bananas are known for their potassium. Potassium helps to reduce blood pressure and supports muscle maintenance. It is also great for "that time of the month" because it is a natural diuretic, which relieves fluid retention and bloating.

Story

I'm not a big fan of chocolate, except for the one time in the month where a girl is at the mercy of her raging hormones! This recipe is a great guilt-free way to indulge. My entire family absolutely loves them. They keep the grumpy mama sane and my boys love it because even though mommy is a grump, they get a treat that they can enjoy. Absolutely delicious!

cherry macaroons

By: Jesse Schelew

Ingredients

1 cup dried cherries

⅓ cup maple syrup

1 tbsp coconut oil, melted

1 tsp vanilla extract

2 cups shredded unsweetened coconut

½ tsp salt (preferably Himalayan rock salt)

CHOCOLATE COATING FOR THE TOP (OPTIONAL)

½ tbsp melted coconut oil

3 tbsp cacao or cocoa powder

½ tbsp maple syrup

Directions

1. Soak cherries in water for 30 minutes to an hour to soften them up.
2. Preheat the oven to 300°F and line a baking sheet with parchment paper or a Silpat.
3. Once the cherries are done soaking, blend them in a food processor with ¼ cup of the soaking water along with maple syrup, coconut oil, and vanilla extract to create a pink paste.
4. In a medium sized bowl mix the shredded coconut and salt into the cherry paste.
5. Scoop 1 tbsp sized balls of dough onto the baking sheet and bake for 25 minutes, or until the bottom of the macaroons are golden brown. You can place the macaroons fairly close together because their shape won't change while cooking.
6. Remove the macaroons from the oven and let them cool for 30 minutes before storing or serving.
7. For the chocolate coating whisk together melted coconut oil, cacao/cocoa powder, and maple syrup and then drizzle on top of macaroons.

Makes roughly 20 macaroons

Nutritional Benefits

Cherries are a great source of antioxidants, which can help lower our risk of heart disease, diabetes, and cancer. They can also help with digestion and sleep. The great thing about baking with coconut oil is that it is a saturated fat that is very stable and can withstand high temperatures without becoming rancid. Also, coconut oil promotes weight loss and is very well absorbed. It is used as an energy source in the body instead of being stored as fat.

Story

As I kid I always loved Valentine's day. A couple days before Valentine's day, my family would decorate a Valentine's day box and when no one was looking, we would slip little love notes to each other into the box. My mom would also put lots of Valentine's day candy in there too, which always went over well. To honor this lovely holiday I wanted to make a festive dessert that was delicious and naturally sweetened. Success!

sexy chocolate torte

By: Tamara Green

Ingredients

- 4 eggs
- ½ cup maple syrup
- ½ cup raw cacao powder or cocoa powder
- ¼ cup coconut oil, melted
- ⅛ tsp sea salt
- ¼ cup dark chocolate chips
- ¼ cup carob chips (optional)
- ¼ cup chopped hazelnuts (optional)

Directions

1. Preheat oven to 350°F.
2. Carefully separate the egg whites from the yolks.
3. Beat the yolks for several minutes, until very thick. Add in ¼ cup maple syrup and beat for another 2 minutes.
4. Stir the cacao/cocoa powder and sea salt into the egg yolks. Add the coconut oil and stir.
5. In a separate bowl, beat the egg whites until peaks form. Beat in the other ¼ cup maple syrup.
6. Carefully fold the egg whites into the yolk mixture. Mix in the chocolate chips and carob chips (if using).
7. Pour into a greased round pie plate (you can use coconut oil to grease it). Sprinkle hazelnuts on top.
8. Bake for 20 minutes, until the center is set.

Serves 6

Nutritional Benefits

This is a decadent recipe that is well balanced. The eggs provide a good source or protein, the coconut oil offers healthy medium-chain fatty-acids that are easily converted into energy in the body, the hazelnuts also provide a great source of healthy fat, and the maple syrup is mineral dense and provides the carbohydrates (glucose) we need for our brain to function. Top this off with antioxidant rich cacao powder and you have a winner!

Story

Sometimes I sit back and realize it's time to celebrate life! We don't always need something big, huge, and spectacular to happen in our life, in order to celebrate. How about celebrating the fact that we are here and breathing and experiencing all that life has to offer? How about making delicious chocolate torte and sharing it with the people we love, while knowing that we are nourishing them with nutrient dense food? Now we're talking! When chocolate cake is involved, I think I could start celebrating life a lot more often!

fiber-rich cookie dough

By: Melissa Ramos

Ingredients

1 ½ cups white beans (1 can, rinsed and drained)

⅛ tsp plus ¹⁄₁₆ tsp salt

¼ tsp baking soda

2 tsp pure vanilla extract

¼ cup hazelnut almond butter

¼ cup unsweetened almond milk

¼ cup–½ cup maple syrup

2 tbsp oats

TOPPING

Cacao nibs or chunks of 80% cacao bar

Directions

1. Add all ingredients (except for cacao nibs) to a food processor and process until combined.
2. Remove and stir in cacao nibs. Let stand for 10 minutes and then serve.

Serves 4

Nutritional Benefits

This fiber-rich dessert is amazing. It's the perfect midnight treat that has a good amount of fiber, fat, and sweetness to let you feel completely satisfied before bed. In addition, the white beans are rich in folate and a great source of tryptophan!

Story

When I was a little girl, I loved cookie dough. I mean, really, who didn't? So when I put this cookie dough recipe together, I wanted to indulge without the guilt. Granted, I realize this has white beans (which you could change up for chickpeas), but you can't even taste them. So go on and feed them to the biggest skeptics and you'll fool every last one of them.

date bliss balls

By: Jesse Schelew

Ingredients

2 cups (roughly 250 g) pitted dates

¼ cup + 2 tbsp warm water

¾ cup oats

¼ cup sesame seeds

¼ cup sunflower seeds

¼ cup chopped almonds

½ cup toasted coconut flakes

½ cup extra coconut flakes for coating

Directions

1. Place dates and warm water in a food processor and process until smooth.
2. Scoop the creamed dates into a bowl and fold in the remaining ingredients (not the extra coconut flakes for coating) until mixed. If the mixture is soggy, then slowly add more oats; alternatively, if the mixture is too dry slowly add warm water.
3. Shape balls between 3 to 4 cm in diameter, roll them in the extra coconut and place on a tray.
4. Place the tray in the freezer for 30 minutes to allow them to set and enjoy straight out of the freezer for a quick energy boost.

Makes roughly 20-25 balls

Nutritional Benefits

Looking for a nutritious dessert or a power snack? Well, look no further! These Date Bliss Balls are naturally sweetened and full of delicious and nutritious seeds and nuts. They are packed with protein and fiber to give you energy to keep going. Perfect for a mid-afternoon pick me up, a before the gym snack, or a sweet treat to finish a meal. No baking is required!

Story

I love doing yoga. Things are often really busy in my life so I am constantly looking for quick snack ideas that I can grab on the go, especially when I'm heading out the door to yoga. I find that having a quick snack about 30 minutes before helps boost my energy for a great class. These little date balls are one of my favorite snacks because they are easy to make ahead of time, store in the freezer, and then grab quickly when I'm running out the door. They also make a great dessert for those times you feel like something sweet after a meal.

wild blueberry tart

By: Marni Wasserman

Ingredients

PIE CRUST

1 cup almonds, roasted and cooled

¾–1 cup oat flour

2 tbsp maple crystals or coconut sugar

¼ tsp baking powder

Pinch of sea salt

3 tbsp melted coconut oil + more for oiling the pan

¼ cup maple syrup

FILLING

2 tbsp agar flakes (natural form of gelatin)

1 ¾ cups apple juice

2 tbsp tapioca (or cornstarch) dissolved in ¼ cup apple juice

2 tbsp maple syrup

Pinch of sea salt

2 cups fresh wild blueberries, washed and drained

Fresh mint to garnish

Directions

Preheat oven to 350°F. Oil a 9" tart pan.

FOR THE CRUST:

1. In food processor, grind nuts to a meal. In mixing bowl, combine nuts, flour, maple crystals, baking powder, and salt.

2. In separate small bowl, whisk together oil and maple syrup.

3. Mix wet ingredients (oil and syrup) into dry ingredients.

4. Press crust mixture into tart pan. Refrigerate for 15–20 minutes, and then bake for 20–25 minutes. Let cool completely.

FOR THE FILLING

1. In a small pot, simmer agar flakes in apple juice until agar completely dissolves. When agar dissolves, add tapioca/juice mixture. Whisk until mixture thickens. Add maple syrup.

2. Add salt and berries. Cook 6–8 minutes. Remove from heat and let mixture cool partially. Pour into cooled crust pan.

3. Let set completely. Garnish with mint before serving. There may be a small amount of filling left, you can enjoy it as a pudding by blending it in a food processor.

Serves 8

Nutritional Benefits

The agar flakes in this recipe help hold the filling ingredients together. They are a tasteless and odorless sea vegetable gelatin that's high in iodine. The crust is made of almonds and oats so it is wheat-free and high in protein and fiber. The blueberries give us a boost of antioxidants.

Story

I was always a berry tart girl. I just loved the glaze that held the berries in place. Of course after learning that "glaze" meant it was gelatin I was quickly turned off. When I discovered the uses of kuzu and agar, I was amazed at how they did the same thing and of course that they were plant based!

hemp fudge

By: Alex Jamieson

Ingredients

2 cups raisins, soaked at least 1 hour in enough water to cover by 2 inches

1 cup shelled hemp seeds

16 oz (454 g) raw tahini (sesame seed butter)

1 cup walnuts, roughly chopped

½ cup cacao powder (or cocoa powder)

¼ cup brown rice syrup

1 tsp ground cinnamon

Pinch of sea salt

Directions

1. Drain the raisins, keeping ½ cup of the soaking water in case you need it for blending.
2. Combine all of the ingredients, except for the soaking water, in a food processor fitted with the standard S-blade. Process until the mixture becomes smooth. You may need to add some liquid to combine the ingredients better, so add 1 tablespoon of the soaking water at a time and blend. You will need to stop and scrape the sides down a few times.
3. Press the mixture into a 9" bread or casserole pan with a rubber spatula.
4. Cover with plastic wrap and refrigerate for at least 2 hours, or overnight, to set.
5. Remove the plastic wrap and cut into pieces and serve.

Makes 24 pieces

Nutritional Benefits

This recipe for hemp fudge is super high in protein and omega-3 fatty acids, thanks to the hemp seeds, raw tahini, and walnuts. The raisins help provide us with energy and the raw cacao powder helps to boost our metabolism, increase the activity of the neurotransmitters in our brain, and tastes really yummy!

Story

If your child is allergic to walnuts like mine, just replace with chopped almonds or skip the added nuts altogether. This recipe was a hit at my Hemp History Week cooking class, and the audience especially liked that it's gluten-free, dairy-free, and super easy!

chia seed pudding with coconut and vanilla

By: Alex Jamieson

Ingredients

2 cups coconut, rice, or hemp milk

1 tsp vanilla extract

2 tbsp brown rice syrup or maple syrup

Pinch of sea salt

¼ cup chia seeds

½ tsp ground cinnamon

Directions

1. Heat the milk over medium heat in a small saucepan.
2. Whisk in the vanilla, brown rice syrup or maple syrup, and sea salt.
3. Once the milk is almost to a simmer, whisk in the chia seeds and cinnamon. Remove from heat and set aside for 15 minutes, or until the mixture gels up to a tapioca consistency.
4. Serve warm, at room temperature, or cool from the refrigerator.

Serves 2–3

Nutritional Benefits

Chia seeds provide us with a large amount of energy and are a great source of fiber, which is important because most adults in North America are not consuming enough daily. These seeds also provide us with a plant source of essential fatty acids, which can help our skin look soft and supple. The addition of cinnamon helps support blood sugar.

Story

I've always loved tapioca pudding, but not the mess... or the crummy ingredients! Chia pudding is super easy to make, and really healthy. I've even eaten this for breakfast, and have no trouble giving it to my son!

I hope you enjoyed getting naked in the kitchen!

For more great recipes, healthy restaurant reviews, and to see which products we have undressed this week, check out:

TheNakedLabel.com

Facebook.com/TheNakedLabel

@TheNakedLabel

CPSIA information can be obtained
at www.ICGtesting.com
Printed in the USA
LVIC01n2021210114
370365LV00014B/174